Blue-grass and Rhododendron

Out-doors in Old Kentucky

By

John Fox, Jr.

Charles Scribner's Sons
New York :::::::::: 1901

Copyright, 1901, by
Charles Scribner's Sons

Published, October, 1901

Trow Directory
Printing & Bookbinding Company
New York

To

JOSHUA F. BULLITT
HENRY CLAY McDOWELL
HORACE ETHELBERT FOX

THE
FIRST THREE CAPTAINS
OF
THE GUARD

Contents

	Page
The Southern Mountaineer	1
The Kentucky Mountaineer	25
Down the Kentucky on a Raft	55
After Br'er Rabbit in the Blue-grass	77
Through the Bad Bend	101
Fox-Hunting in Kentucky	123
To the Breaks of Sandy	149
Br'er Coon in Ole Kentucky	177
Civilizing the Cumberland	207
The Hanging of Talton Hall	237
The Red Fox of the Mountains	261
Man-Hunting in the Pound	275

List of Illustrations

Melissa . . . . . . *Frontispiece*	
	Page
Interior of a Log-cabin on Brownie's Creek .	8
" Gritting " Corn and Hand Corn-mill . .	16
Breaking Flax near the mouth of Brownie's Creek	22
A Moonshine Still	40
Rockhouse Post-office and Store, Letcher County	48
Ferrying at Jackson, Ky.	58
Down goes her pursuer on top of her . . .	94
The rest of us sat on the two beds . . .	106
Calling off the Dogs	132
Listening to the Music of the Dogs . .	136
A Bit of Brush	142
They took us for the advance-guard of a circus .	158
Along roads scarce wide enough for one wagon .	162
At the Breaks	168
" Go it, Black Babe! Go it, my White Chile!" .	196

List of Illustrations

	Page
The Infant of the Guard	234
Hall stood as motionless as the trunk of an oak	258
Going to Circuit Court	266
"Hev you ever searched for a dead man?"	290

The Southern Mountaineer

IT was only a little while ago that the materialists declared that humanity was the product of heredity and environment; that history lies not *near* but *in* Nature; and that, in consequence, man must take his head from the clouds and study himself with his feet where they belong, to the earth. Since then, mountains have taken on a new importance for the part they have played in the destiny of the race, for the reason that mountains have dammed the streams of humanity, have let them settle in the valleys and spread out over plains; or have sent them on long detours around. When some unusual pressure has forced a current through some mountain-pass, the hills have cut it off from the main stream and have held it so stagnant, that, to change the figure, mountains may be said to have kept the records of human history somewhat as fossils hold the history of the earth.

Arcadia held primitive the primitive inhabitants of Greece, who fled to its rough hills after the Dorian invasion. The Pyrenees kept unconquered and strikingly unchanged the Basques—sole remnants perhaps in western Europe of the aborigines who were swept away by the tides of Aryan immigration; just as the Rocky Mountains protect the American Indian in primitive barbarism and not wholly subdued to-day, and the Cumberland range keeps the Southern mountaineer to the backwoods civilization of the revolution. The reason is plain. The mountain dweller lives apart from the world. The present is the past when it reaches him; and though past, is yet too far in the future to have any bearing on his established order of things. There is, in consequence, no incentive whatever for him to change. An arrest of development follows; so that once imprisoned, a civilization, with its dress, speech, religion, customs, ideas, may be caught like the shapes of lower life in stone, and may tell the human story of a century as the rocks tell the story of an age. For centuries the Highlander has had plaid and kilt; the peasant of Norway and the mountaineer of the German and Austrian Alps each a habit of his own; and every Swiss canton a distinctive dress. Mountains preserve the Gaelic tongue in which the scholar may yet read the refuge of Celt from Saxon, and in turn Saxon from the Norman-French, just as they keep alive remnants like the Rhæto-Roman, the

The Southern Mountaineer

Basque, and a number of Caucasian dialects. The Carpathians protected Christianity against the Moors, and in Java the Brahman faith took refuge on the sides of the Volcano Gunung Lawa, and there outlived the ban of Buddha.

So, in the log-cabin of the Southern mountaineer, in his household furnishings, in his homespun, his linsey, and, occasionally, in his hunting-shirt, his coonskin cap and moccasins, one may summon up the garb and life of the pioneer; in his religion, his politics, his moral code, his folk-songs, and his superstitions, one may bridge the waters back to the old country, and through his speech one may even touch the remote past of Chaucer. For to-day he is a distinct remnant of Colonial times—a distinct relic of an Anglo-Saxon past.

It is odd to think that he was not discovered until the outbreak of the Civil War, although he was nearly a century old then, and it is really startling to realize that when one speaks of the Southern mountaineers, he speaks of nearly three millions of people who live in eight Southern States—Virginia and Alabama and the Southern States between—and occupy a region equal in area to the combined areas of Ohio and Pennsylvania, as big, say, as the German Empire, and richer, perhaps, in timber and mineral deposits than any other region of similar extent in the world. This region was

Blue-grass and Rhododendron

and is an unknown land. It has been aptly called "Appalachian America," and the work of discovery is yet going on. The American mountaineer was discovered, I say, at the beginning of the war, when the Confederate leaders were counting on the presumption that Mason and Dixon's Line was the dividing line between the North and South, and formed, therefore, the plan of marching an army from Wheeling, in West Virginia, to some point on the lakes, and thus dissevering the North at one blow. The plan seemed so feasible that it is said to have materially aided the sale of Confederate bonds in England, but when Captain Garnett, a West Point graduate, started to carry it out, he got no farther than Harper's Ferry. When he struck the mountains, he struck enemies who shot at his men from ambush, cut down bridges before him, carried the news of his march to the Federals, and Garnett himself fell with a bullet from a mountaineer's squirrel rifle at Harper's Ferry. Then the South began to realize what a long, lean, powerful arm of the Union it was that the Southern mountaineer stretched through its very vitals; for that arm helped hold Kentucky in the Union by giving preponderance to the Union sympathizers in the Blue-grass; it kept the East Tennesseans loyal to the man; it made West Virginia, as the phrase goes, "secede from secession"; it drew

The Southern Mountaineer

out a horde of one hundred thousand volunteers, when Lincoln called for troops, depleting Jackson County, Ky., for instance, of every male under sixty years of age and over fifteen, and it raised a hostile barrier between the armies of the coast and the armies of the Mississippi. The North has never realized, perhaps, what it owes for its victory to this non-slaveholding Southern mountaineer.

The war over, he went back to his cove and his cabin, and but for the wealth of his hills and the pen of one Southern woman, the world would have forgotten him again. Charles Egbert Craddock put him in the outer world of fiction, and in recent years railroads have been linking him with the outer world of fact. Religious and educational agencies have begun work on him; he has increased in political importance, and a few months ago he went down, heavily armed with pistol and Winchester—a thousand strong—to assert his political rights in the State capital of Kentucky. It was probably one of these mountaineers who killed William Goebel, and he no doubt thought himself as much justified as any other assassin who ever slew the man he thought a tyrant. Being a Unionist, because of the Revolution, a Republican, because of the Civil War, and having his antagonism aroused against the Blue-grass people, who, he believes, are trying to rob him of his liberties, he is now the political factor with which the Anti-Goebel Democrats—in all ways the best element in the State—have imperilled the Democratic Party in Kentucky. Sooner or later, there will be an awakening in the mountainous parts of the seven other States; already the coal and iron of these regions are making many a Southern ear listen to the plea of protection; and some day the National Democratic Party will, like the Confederacy, find a subtle and powerful foe in the Southern mountaineer and in the riches of his hills.

In the march of civilization westward, the Southern mountaineer has been left in an isolation almost beyond belief. He was shut off by mountains that have blocked and still block the commerce of a century, and there for a century he has stayed. He has had no navigable rivers, no lakes, no coasts, few wagon-roads, and often no roads at all except the beds of streams. He has lived in the cabin in which his grandfather was born, and in life, habit, and thought he has been merely his grandfather born over again. The first generation after the Revolution had no schools and no churches. Both are rare and primitive to-day. To this day, few Southern mountaineers can read and write and cipher; few, indeed, can do more. They saw little of the newspapers, and were changeless in politics as

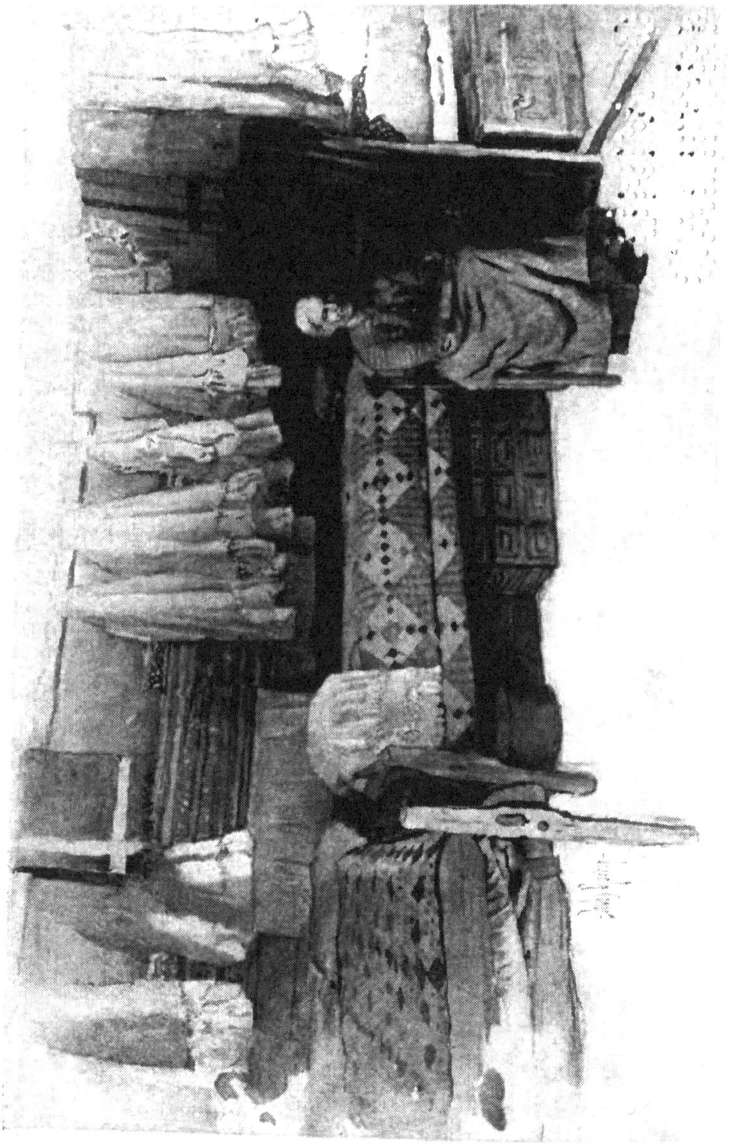

The Southern Mountaineer

in everything else. They cared little for what was going on in the outside world, and indeed they heard nothing that did not shake the nation. To the average mountaineer, the earth was still flat and had four corners. It was the sun that girdled the earth, just as it did when Joshua told it to stand still, and precisely for that reason. The stories of votes yet being cast for Andrew Jackson are but little exaggerated. An old Tennessee mountaineer once told me about the discovery of America by Columbus. He could read his Bible, with marvellous interpretations of the same. He was the patriarch of his district, the philosopher. He had acquired the habit of delivering the facts of modern progress to his fellows, and it never occurred to him that a man of my youth might be acquainted with that rather well-known bit of history. I listened gravely, and he went on, by and by, to speak of the Mexican War as we would speak of the fighting in China; and when we got down to so recent and burning an issue as the late civil struggle, he dropped his voice to a whisper and hitched his chair across the fireplace and close to mine.

"Some folks had other idees," he said, "but hit's my pussonal opinion that *niggahs was the cause o' the war.*"

When I left his cabin, he followed me out to the fence.

Blue-grass and Rhododendron

"Stranger," he said, "I'd ruther you wouldn' say nothin' about whut I been tellin' ye." He had been a lone rebel in sympathy, and he feared violence at this late day for expressing his opinion too freely. This old man was a "citizen"; I was a "furriner" from the "settlements"—that is, the Blue-grass. Columbus was one of the "outlandish," a term that carried not only his idea of the parts hailed from but his personal opinion of Columbus. Living thus, his interest centred in himself, his family, his distant neighbor, his grist-mill, his country store, his county town; unaffected by other human influences; having no incentive to change, no wish for it, and remaining therefore unchanged, except where civilization during the last decade has pressed in upon him, the Southern mountaineer is thus practically the pioneer of the Revolution, the living ancestor of the Modern West.

The national weapons of the pioneer—the axe and the rifle—are the Southern mountaineer's weapons to-day. He has still the same fight with Nature. His cabin was, and is yet, in many places, the cabin of the backwoodsman—of one room usually—sometimes two, connected by a covered porch, and built of unhewn logs, with a puncheon floor, clapboards for shingles, and wooden pin and auger-holes for nails. The crevices between the logs were filled with mud and stones

The Southern Mountaineer

when filled at all, and there were holes in the roof for the wind and the rain. Sometimes there was a window with a batten wooden shutter, sometimes no window at all. Over the door, across a pair of buck antlers, lay the long, heavy, home-made rifle of the backwoodsman, sometimes even with a flint lock. One can yet find a crane swinging in a big stone fireplace, the spinning-wheel and the loom in actual use; sometimes the hominy block that the pioneers borrowed from the Indians, and a hand-mill for grinding corn like the one, perhaps, from which one woman was taken and another left in biblical days. Until a decade and a half ago they had little money, and the medium of exchange was barter. They drink metheglin still, as well as moonshine. They marry early, and only last summer I saw a fifteen-year-old girl riding behind her father, to a log church, to be married. After the service her pillion was shifted to her young husband's horse, as was the pioneer custom, and she rode away behind him to her new home. There are still log-rollings, house-raisings, house-warmings, corn-shuckings, and quiltings. Sports are still the same—as they have been for a hundred years—wrestling, racing, jumping, and lifting barrels. Brutally savage fights are still common in which the combatants strike, kick, bite, and gouge until one is ready to cry "enough."

Blue-grass and Rhododendron

Even the backwoods bully, loud, coarse, profane, bantering—a dandy who wore long hair and embroidered his hunting-shirt with porcupine-quills—is not quite dead. I saw one not long since, but he wore store clothes, a gorgeous red tie, a dazzling brass scarf-pin—in the bosom of his shirt. His hair was sandy, but his mustache was blackened jet. He had the air and smirk of a lady-killer, and in the butt of the huge pistol buckled around him was a large black bow—the badge of death and destruction to his enemies. Funerals are most simple. Sometimes the coffin is slung to poles and carried by four men. While the begum has given place to hickory bark when a cradle is wanted, baskets and even fox-horns are still made of that material.

Not only many remnants like these are left in the life of the mountaineer, but, occasionally, far up some creek, it was possible, as late as fifteen years ago, to come upon a ruddy, smooth-faced, big-framed old fellow, keen-eyed, taciturn, avoiding the main-travelled roads; a great hunter, calling his old squirrel rifle by some pet feminine name—who, with a coonskin cap, the scalp in front, and a fringed hunting-shirt and moccasins, completed the perfect image of the pioneer as the books and tradition have handed him down to us.

The Southern Mountaineer

It is easy to go on back across the water to the Old Country. One finds still among the mountaineers the pioneer's belief in signs, omens, and the practice of witchcraft; for whatever traits the pioneer brought over the sea, the Southern mountaineer has to-day. The rough-and-tumble fight of the Scotch and the English square stand-up and knock-down boxing-match were the mountaineer's ways of settling minor disputes—one or the other, according to agreement —until the war introduced musket and pistol. The imprint of Calvinism on his religious nature is yet plain, in spite of the sway of Methodism for nearly a century. He is the only man in the world whom the Catholic Church has made little or no effort to proselyte. Dislike of Episcopalianism is still strong among people who do not know, or pretend not to know, what the word means.

"Any Episcopalians around here?" asked a clergyman at a mountain cabin. "I don' know," said the old woman. "Jim's got the skins of a lot o' varmints up in the loft. Mebbe you can find one up thar."

The Unionism of the mountaineer in the late war is in great part an inheritance from the intense Americanism of the backwoodsman, just as that Americanism came from the spirit of the Covenanters. His music is thus a trans-Atlantic remnant. In Harlan County,

Blue-grass and Rhododendron

Ky., a mountain girl leaned her chair against the wall of her cabin, put her large, bare feet on one of the rungs, and sang me an English ballad three hundred years old, and almost as long as it was ancient. She said she knew many others. In Perry County, where there are in the French-Eversole feud McIntyres, McIntoshes, McKnights, Combs, probably McCombs and Fitzpatricks, Scotch ballads are said to be sung with Scotch accent, and an occasional copy of Burns is to be found. I have even run across the modern survival of the wandering minstrel—two blind fiddlers who went through the mountains making up "ballets" to celebrate the deeds of leaders in Kentucky feuds. One of the verses ran:

> The death of these two men
> Caused great trouble in our land,
> Caused men to say the bitter word,
> And take the parting hand.

Nearly all songs and dance tunes are written in the so-called old Scotch scale, and, like negro music, they drop frequently into the relative minor; so that if there be any truth in the theory that negro music is merely the adaptation of Scotch and Irish folksongs, and folk-dances, with the added stamp of the negro's peculiar temperament, then the music

The Southern Mountaineer

adapted is to be heard in the mountains to-day as the negro heard it long ago.

In his speech the mountaineer touches a very remote past. Strictly speaking, he has no dialect. The mountaineer simply keeps in use old words and meanings that the valley people have ceased to use; but nowhere is this usage so sustained and consistent as to form a dialect. To writers of mountain stories the temptation seems quite irresistible to use more peculiar words in one story than can be gathered from the people in a month. Still, unusual words are abundant. There are perhaps two hundred words, meanings, and pronunciations that in the mountaineer's speech go back unchanged to Chaucer. Some of the words are: afeerd, afore, axe, holp, crope, clomb, peert, beest (horse), cryke, eet (ate), farwel, fer (far), fool (foolish —" them fool-women "), heepe, hit (it), I is, lepte, pore (poor), right (very), slyk, study (think), souple (supple), up (verb), " he up and done it," usen, yer for year, yond, instid, yit, etc. There are others which have English dialect authority: blather, doated, antic, dreen, brash, faze (now modern slang), fernent, ferninst, master, size, etc. Many of these words, of course, the upper classes use throughout the South. These, the young white master got from his negro playmates, who took them from the lips of the poor whites.

Blue-grass and Rhododendron

The double negative, always used by the old English, who seem to have resisted it no more than did the Greeks, is invariable with the mountaineer. With him a triple negative is common. A mountaineer had been shot. His friends came in to see him and kept urging him to revenge. A woman wanted them to stop.

" Hit jes' raises the ambition in him and *don't* do *no* good *nohow*."

The " dialect " is not wholly deterioration, then. What we are often apt to regard as ignorance in the mountaineer is simply our own disuse. Unfortunately, the speech is a mixture of so many old English dialects that it is of little use in tracing the origin of the people who use it.

Such has been the outward protective effect of mountains on the Southern mountaineer. As a human type he is of unusual interest.

No mountain people are ever rich. Environment keeps mountaineers poor. The strength that comes from numbers and wealth is always wanting. Agriculture is the sole stand-by, and agriculture distributes population, because arable soil is confined to bottom-lands and valleys. Farming on a mountain-side is not only arduous and unremunerative—it is sometimes dangerous. There is a well-authenticated case of a

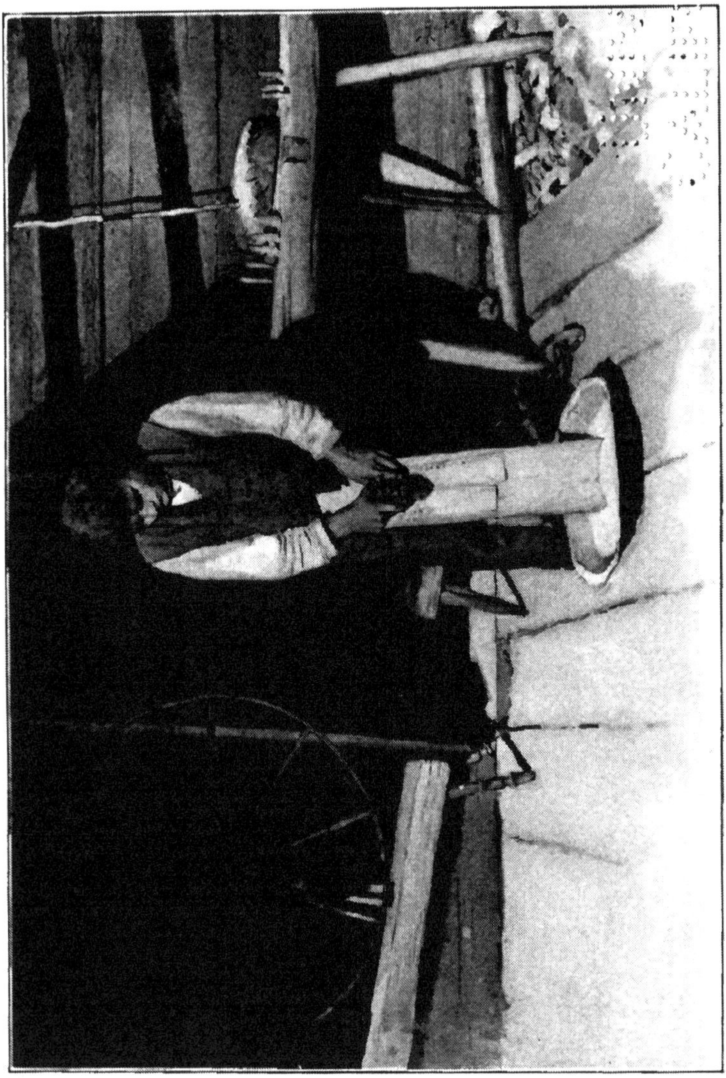

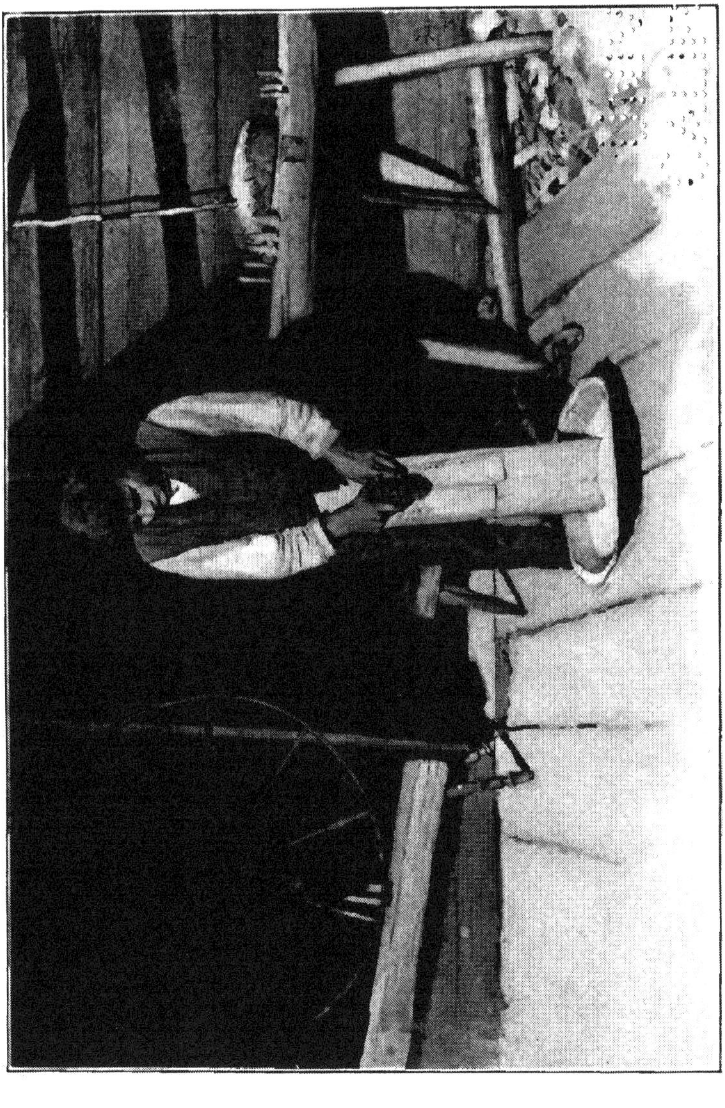

The Southern Mountaineer

Kentucky mountaineer who fell out of his own cornfield and broke his neck. Still, though fairly well-to-do in the valleys, the Southern mountaineer can be pathetically poor. A young preacher stopped at a cabin in Georgia to stay all night. His hostess, as a mark of unusual distinction, killed a chicken and dressed it in a pan. She rinsed the pan and made up her dough in it. She rinsed it again and went out and used it for a milk-pail. She came in, rinsed it again, and went to the spring and brought it back full of water. She filled up the glasses on the table and gave him the pan with the rest of the water in which to wash his hands. The woman was not a slattern; it was the only utensil she had.

This poverty of natural resources makes the mountaineer's fight for life a hard one. At the same time it gives him vigor, hardihood, and endurance of body; it saves him from the comforts and dainties that weaken; and it makes him a formidable competitor, when it forces him to come down into the plains, as it often does. For this poverty was at the bottom of the marauding instinct of the Pict and Scot, just as it is at the bottom of the migrating instinct that sends the Southern mountaineers west, in spite of a love for home that is a proverb with the Swiss, and is hardly less strong in the Southern mountaineer to-day. In-

Blue-grass and Rhododendron

variably the Western wanderer comes home again. Time and again an effort was made to end a feud in the Kentucky mountains by sending the leaders away. They always came back.

It is this poverty of arable land that further isolates the mountaineer in his loneliness. For he must live apart not only from the world, but from his neighbor. The result is an enforced self-reliance, and through that, the gradual growth of an individualism that has been " the strength, the weakness; the personal charm, the political stumbling-block; the ethical significance and the historical insignificance of the mountaineer the world over." It is this isolation, this individualism, that makes unity of action difficult, public sentiment weak, and takes from the law the righting of private wrongs. It is this individualism that has been a rich mine for the writer of fiction. In the Southern mountaineer, its most marked elements are religious feeling, hospitality, and pride. So far these last two traits have been lightly touched upon, for the reason that they appear only by contrast with a higher civilization that has begun to reach them only in the last few years.

The latch-string hangs outside every cabin-door if the men-folks are at home, but you must shout " hello " always outside the fence.

The Southern Mountaineer

"We uns is pore," you will be told, "but y'u're welcome ef y'u kin put up with what we have."

After a stay of a week at a mountain cabin, a young "furriner" asked what his bill was. The old mountaineer waved his hand. "Nothin'," he said, "'cept come agin!"

A belated traveller asked to stay all night at a cabin. The mountaineer answered that his wife was sick and they were "sorter out o' fixin's to eat, but he reckoned he mought step over to a neighbor's an borrer some." He did step over and he was gone three hours. He brought back a little bag of meal, and they had cornbread and potatoes for supper and for breakfast, cooked by the mountaineer. The stranger asked how far away his next neighbor lived. "A leetle the rise o' six miles I reckon," was the answer.

"Which way?"

"Oh, jes' over the mountain thar."

He had stepped six miles over the mountain and back for that little bag of meal, and he would allow his guest to pay nothing next morning.

I have slept with nine others in a single room. The host gave up his bed to two of our party, and he and his wife slept with the rest of us on the floor. He gave us supper, kept us all night, sent us away next morning with a parting draught of moonshine apple-jack, of

Blue-grass and Rhododendron

his own brewing, by the way, and would suffer no one to pay a cent for his entertainment. That man was a desperado, an outlaw, a moonshiner, and was running from the sheriff at that very time.

Two outlaw sons were supposed to be killed by officers. I offered aid to the father to have them decently clothed and buried, but the old man, who was as bad as his sons, declined it with some dignity. They had enough left for that; and if not, why, he had.

A woman whose husband was dead, who was sick to death herself, whose four children were almost starved, said, when she heard the "furriners" were talking about sending her to the poor-house, that she " would go out on her crutches and hoe corn fust" (and she did), and that "people who talked about sending her to the po'-house had better save their breath to make prayers with."

It is a fact—in the Kentucky mountains at least—that the poor-houses are usually empty, and that it is considered a disgrace to a whole clan if one of its members is an inmate. It is the exception when a family is low and lazy enough to take a revenue from the State for an idiot child. I saw a boy once, astride a steer which he had bridled with a rope, barefooted, with his yellow hair sticking from his crownless hat, and in blubbering ecstasy over the fact that he was

The Southern Mountaineer

no longer under the humiliation of accepting $75 a year from the State. He had proven his sanity by his answer to one question.

"Do you work in the field?" asked the commissioner.

"Well, ef I didn't," was the answer, "thar wouldn't be no work done."

I have always feared, however, that there was another reason for his happiness than balm to his suffering pride. Relieved of the ban of idiocy, he had gained a privilege—unspeakably dear in the mountains—the privilege of matrimony.

Like all mountain races, the Southern mountaineers are deeply religious. In some communities, religion is about the only form of recreation they have. They are for the most part Methodists and Baptists—sometimes Ironsides feet-washing Baptists. They will walk, or ride when possible, eight or ten miles, and sit all day in a close, windowless log-cabin on the flat side of a slab supported by pegs, listening to the highwrought, emotional, and, at times, unintelligible ranting of a mountain preacher, while the young men sit outside, whittling with their Barlows and huge jackknives, and swapping horses and guns.

"If anybody wants to extribute anything to the export of the gospels, hit will be gradually received." A possible remark of this sort will gauge the intelligence of the pastor. The cosmopolitanism of the congregation can be guessed from the fact that certain elders, filling a vacancy in their pulpit, once decided to "take that ar man Spurgeon if they could git him to come." It is hardly necessary to add that the "extribution to the export of the gospels" is very, very gradually received.

Naturally, their religion is sternly orthodox and most literal. The infidel is unknown, and no mountaineer is so bad as not to have a full share of religion deep down, though, as in his more civilized brother, it is not always apparent until death is at hand. In the famous Howard and Turner war, the last but one of the Turner brothers was shot by a Howard while he was drinking at a spring. He leaped to his feet and fell in a little creek, where, from behind a sycamore-root, he emptied his Winchester at his enemy, and between the cracks of his gun he could be heard, half a mile away, praying aloud.

The custom of holding funeral services for the dead annually, for several years after death, is common. I heard the fourth annual funeral sermon of a dead feud leader preached a few summers ago, and it was consoling to hear that even he had all the virtues that so few men seem to have in life, and so few to lack

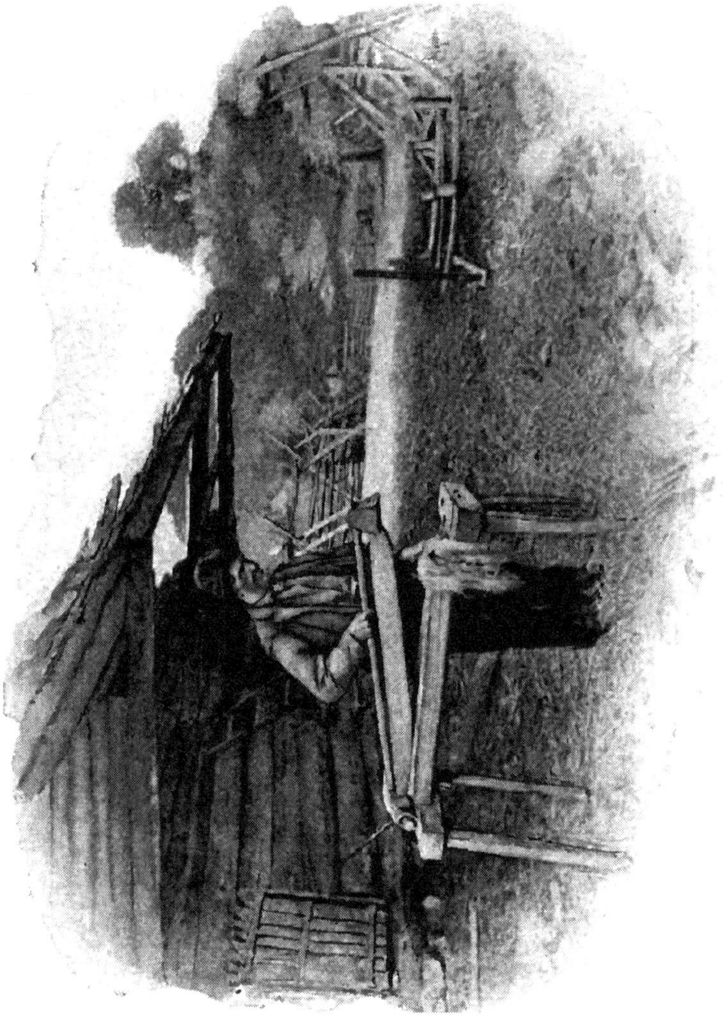

The Southern Mountaineer

when dead. But in spite of the universality of religious feeling and a surprising knowledge of the Bible, it is possible to find an ignorance that is almost incredible. The mountain evangelist, George O. Barnes, it is said, once stopped at a mountain cabin and told the story of the crucifixion as few other men can. When he was quite through, an old woman who had listened in absorbed silence, asked:

"Stranger, you say that that happened a long while ago?"

"Yes," said Mr. Barnes; "almost two thousand years ago."

"And they treated him that way when he'd come down fer nothin' on earth but to save 'em?"

"Yes."

The old woman was crying softly, and she put out her hand and laid it on his knee.

"Well, stranger," she said, "let's hope that hit ain't so."

She did not want to believe that humanity was capable of such ingratitude. While ignorance of this kind is rare, and while we may find men who know the Bible from "kiver to kiver," it is not impossible to find children of shrewd native intelligence who have not heard of Christ and the Bible.

Now, whatever interest the Southern mountaineer

Blue-grass and Rhododendron

has as a remnant of pioneer days, as a relic of an Anglo-Saxon past, and as a peculiar type that seems to be the invariable result of a mountain environment—the Kentucky mountaineer shares in a marked degree. Moreover, he has an interest peculiarly his own; for I believe him to be as sharply distinct from his fellows, as the blue-grass Kentuckian is said to be from his.

The Kentucky Mountaineer

THE Kentucky mountaineers are practically valley people. There are the three forks of the Cumberland, the three forks of the Kentucky, and the tributaries of Big Sandy—all with rich river-bottoms. It was natural that these lands should attract a better class of people than the average mountaineer. They did. There were many slaveholders among them—a fact that has never been mentioned, as far as I know, by anybody who has written about the mountaineer. The houses along these rivers are, as a rule, weather-boarded, and one will often find interior decorations, startling in color and puzzling in design, painted all over porch, wall, and ceiling. The people are better fed, better clothed, less lank in figure, more intelligent. They wear less homespun, and their speech, while as archaic as elsewhere, is, I believe, purer. You rarely hear " you uns " and " we uns," and similar untraceable confusions in the Kentucky mountains, except along the border of the Tennessee. Moreover, the mountaineers who came over from West Virginia and from the southwestern corner of old Virginia were undoubtedly the daring, the hardy, and the strong, for no other kind would have climbed gloomy Black Mountain and the Cumberland Range to fight against beast and savage for their homes.

However, in spite of the general superiority that these facts give him, the Kentucky mountaineer has been more isolated than the mountaineer of any other State. There are regions more remote and more sparsely settled, but nowhere in the Southern mountains has so large a body of mountaineers been shut off so completely from the outside world. As a result, he illustrates Mr. Theodore Roosevelt's fine observation that life away from civilization simply emphasizes the natural qualities, good and bad, of the individual. The effect of this truth seems perceptible in that any trait common to the Southern mountaineer seems to be intensified in the mountaineer of Kentucky. He is more clannish, prouder, more hospitable, fiercer, more loyal as a friend, more bitter as an enemy, and in simple meanness—when he is mean, mind you—he can out-Herod his race with great ease.

To illustrate his clannishness: Three mountaineers with a grievance went up to some mines to drive the book-keeper away. A fourth man joined them and stood with drawn pistol during the controversy at the mines, because his wife was a first cousin by marriage of one of the three who had the grievance. In Republican counties, county officers are often Democratic —blood is a stronger tie even than politics.

As to his hospitality: A younger brother of mine was taking dinner with an old mountaineer. There was nothing on the table but some bread and a few potatoes.

"Take out, stranger," he said, heartily. "Have a 'tater—take two of 'em—take damn nigh all of 'em!"

A mountaineer, who had come into possession of a small saw-mill, was building a new house. As he had plenty of lumber, a friend of mine asked why he did not build a bigger house. It was big enough, he said. He had two rooms—" one fer the family, an' t'other fer company." As his family numbered fifteen, the scale on which he expected to entertain can be imagined.

The funeral sermon of a mountaineer, who had been dead two years, was preached in Turkey Foot at the base of Mount Scratchum in Jackson County. Three branches run together like a turkey's foot at that point. The mountain is called Scratchum because it is hard to climb. "A funeral sermon," said the old preacher,

Blue-grass and Rhododendron

"can be the last one you hear, or the fust one that's preached over ye atter death. Maybe I'm a-preachin' my own funeral sermon now." If he was, he did himself justice, for he preached three solid hours. The audience was invited to stay to dinner. Forty of them accepted—there were just forty there—and dinner was served from two o'clock until six. The forty were pressed to stay all night. Twenty-three did stay, seventeen in one room. Such is the hospitality of the Kentucky mountaineer.

As to his pride, that is almost beyond belief. I always hesitate to tell this story, for the reason that I can hardly believe it myself. There was a plague in the mountains of eastern Kentucky, West Virginia, and the southwest corner of old Virginia in 1885. A cattle convention of St. Louis made up a relief fund and sent it for distribution to General Jubal Early of Virginia. General Early sent it to a lawyer of Abingdon, Va., who persuaded D. F. Campbell, another lawyer now living in that town, to take the money into the mountains. Campbell left several hundred dollars in Virginia, and being told that the West Virginians could take care of themselves went with the balance, about $1,000, into Kentucky, where the plague was at its worst. He found the suffering great—nine dead, in one instance, under a single roof.

The Kentucky Mountaineer

He spent one month going from house to house in the counties of Letcher, Perry, and Pike, carrying the money in his saddle-bags and riding unarmed. Every man, woman, and child in the three counties knew he had the money and knew his mission. He left $5 at a country store, and he got one woman to persuade another woman whose husband and three children were just dead, and who had indignantly refused his personal offer of assistance, to accept $10. The rest of the money he took back and distributed without trouble on his own side of the mountain.

While in Kentucky he found trouble in getting enough to eat for himself and his horse. Often he had only bread and onions; and yet he was permitted to pay but for one meal for either, and that was under protest at a regular boarding-house in a mountain town. Over the three counties, he got the same answer.

"You are a stranger. We are not beggars, and we can take care of ourselves."

"They are a curious people over there," said Campbell, who is a born Virginian. "No effort was made to rob me, though a man who was known as 'the only thief in Perry County,' a man whom I know to have been trusted with large sums by his leader in a local war, sent me a joking threat. The people were not suspicious of me because I was a stranger. They concealed cases of suffering from me. It was pride that made them refuse the money—nothing else. They are the most loyal friends you ever saw. They will do anything for you, if they like you. They will get up and go anywhere for you day or night, rain or snow. If they haven't a horse, they'll walk. If they haven't shoes, they'll go barefooted. They will combine against you in a trade, and take every advantage they can. A man will keep you at his house to beat you out of a dollar, and when you leave, your board-bill is nothing."

This testimony is from a Virginian, and it is a particular pleasure for a representative of one of the second-class families of Virginia who, as the first families say, all emigrated to Kentucky, to prove, by the word of a Virginian, that we have some advantage in at least one section of the State.

Indeed, no matter what may be said of the mountaineer in general, the Kentucky mountaineer seems to go the fact one better. Elsewhere, families are large —"children and heepe," says Chaucer. In Jackson County a mountaineer died not long ago, not at an extreme old age, who left two hundred and seven descendants. He had fifteen children, and several of his children had fifteen. There was but one set of twins among them—both girls—and they were called

The Kentucky Mountaineer

Louisa and Louīsa. There is in the same county a woman forty-seven years of age, with a grand-daughter who has been married fifteen months. Only a break in the family tradition prevented her from being a great-grandmother at forty-seven.

It may be that the Kentucky mountaineer is more tempted to an earlier marriage than is the mountaineer elsewhere, for an artist who rode with me through the Kentucky mountains said that not only were the men finer looking, but that the women were far handsomer than elsewhere in the southern Alleghanies. While I am not able to say this, I can say that in the Kentucky mountains the pretty mountain girl is not always, as some people are inclined to believe, pure fiction. Pretty girls are, however, rare; for usually the women are stoop-shouldered and large waisted from working in the fields and lifting heavy weights; for the same reason their hands are large and so are their feet, for they generally go barefoot. But usually they have modest faces and sad, modest eyes, and in the rich river-bottoms, where the mountain farmers have tenants and do not send their daughters to the fields, the girls are apt to be erect and agile, small of hand and foot, and usually they have a wild shyness that is very attractive. I recall one girl in crimson homespun, with very big dark eyes, slipping like a

Blue-grass and Rhododendron

flame through the dark room, behind me, when I was on the porch; or gliding out of the one door, if I chanced to enter the other, which I did at every opportunity. A friend who was with me saw her dancing in the dust at twilight, next day, when she was driving the cows home. He helped her to milk and got to know her quite well, I believe. I know that, a year later, when she had worn away her shyness and most of her charm at school in her county seat, she asked me about him, with embarrassing frankness, and a look crept into her eyes that told an old tale. Pretty girls there are in abundance, but I have seen only one very beautiful mountain girl. One's standard can be affected by a long stay in the mountains, and I should have distrusted mine had it not been for the artist who was with me, fresh from civilization. We saw her, as we were riding up the Cumberland, and we silently and simultaneously drew rein and asked if we could get buttermilk. We could, and we swung from our horses. The girl was sitting behind a little cabin, with a baby in her lap, and her loveliness was startling. She was slender; her hair was gold-brown; her hands were small and, for a wonder, beautifully shaped. Her teeth, for a wonder, too, were very white and even. Her features were delicately perfect; her mouth shaped as Cupid's bow never was and never

The Kentucky Mountaineer

would be, said the artist, who christened her eyes after Trilby's—"twin gray stars"—to which the eyebrows and the long lashes gave an indescribable softness. But I felt more the brooding pathos that lay in them, that came from generations of lonely mothers before her, waiting in lonely cabins for the men to come home —back to those wild pioneer days, when they watched with an ever-present fear that they might not come at all.

It was late and we tried to get to stay all night, for the artist wanted to sketch her. He was afraid to ask her permission on so short an acquaintance, for she would not have understood, and he would have frightened her. Her mother gave us buttermilk and we furtively studied her, but we could not stay all night: there were no men-folks at home and no "roughness" for our horses, and we rode regretfully away.

Now, while the good of the mountaineer is emphasized in the mountaineer of Kentucky, the evil is equally marked. The Kentucky mountaineer may be the best of all—he *can* be likewise the worst of all.

A mountaineer was under indictment for moonshining in a little mountain town that has been under the refining influence of a railroad for several years. Unable to give bond, he was ordered to jail by the

Blue-grass and Rhododendron

judge. When the sheriff rose, a huge mountaineer rose, too, in the rear of the court-room and whipped out a big revolver. "You come with me," he said, and the prisoner came, while judge, jury, and sheriff watched him march out. The big fellow took the prisoner through the town and a few hundred yards up a creek. "You go on home," he said. Then the rescuer went calmly back to his house in town, and nothing further has been said or done to this day. The mountaineer was a United States deputy marshal, but the prisoner was his friend.

This marshal was one of the most picturesque figures in the mountains. When sober, he was kind-hearted, good-tempered, and gentle; and always he was fearless and cool. Once, while firing at two assailants who were shooting at him, he stopped long enough to blow his nose deliberately, and then calmly went on shooting again. He had a companion at arms who, singularly enough, came from the North, and occasionally these two would amuse themselves. When properly exhilarated, one would put a horse-collar on the other, and hitch him to an open buggy. He would fill the buggy with pistols, climb in, and drive around the court-house—each man firing off a pistol with each hand and yelling himself hoarse. Then they would execute an Indian war-dance in the court-house square—firing their pistols alternately into the ground and into the air. The town looked on silently and with great respect, and the two were most exemplary until next time.

A superintendent of some mines near a mountain town went to the mayor one Sunday morning to get permission to do some work that had to be done in the town limits that day. He found the august official in his own jail. Exhilaration!

It was at these mines that three natives of the town went up to drive two young men into the bushes. Being met with some firmness and the muzzle of a Winchester, they went back for reinforcements. One of the three was a member of a famous fighting clan, and he gave it out that he was going for his friends to make the "furriners" leave the country. The young men appealed to the town for protection for themselves and property. There was not an officer to answer. The sheriff was in another part of the county and the constable had just resigned. The young men got Winchester repeating shot-guns and waited a week for their assailants, who failed to come; but had they been besieged, there would not have been a soul to give them assistance, except perhaps the marshal and his New England friend.

In this same county a man hired an assassin to kill

his rival. The assassin crept to the window of the house where the girl lived, and, seeing a man sitting by the fire, shot through the window and killed him. It was the wrong man. Assassinations from ambush have not been uncommon in every feud, though, in almost every feud, there has been one faction that refused to fight except in the open. I have even heard of a snare being set for a woman, who, though repeatedly warned, persisted in carrying news from one side to the other. A musket was loaded with slugs and placed so that the discharge would sweep the path that it was believed she would take. A string was tied to the trigger and stretched across the foot road and a mountaineer waited under a bluff to whistle, so that she would stop, when she struck the string. That night the woman happened to take another path. This, however, is the sole instance I have ever known.

Elsewhere the Southern mountaineer holds human life as cheap; elsewhere he is ready to let death settle a personal dispute; elsewhere he is more ignorant and has as little regard for law; elsewhere he was divided against himself by the war and was left in subsequent conditions just as lawless; elsewhere he has similar clannishness of feeling, and elsewhere is an occasional feud which is confined to family and close kindred. But nowhere is the feud so common, so

The Kentucky Mountaineer

old, so persistent, so deadly, as in the Kentucky mountains. Nowhere else is there such organization, such division of enmity to the limit of kinship.

About thirty-five years ago two boys were playing marbles in the road along the Cumberland River—down in the Kentucky mountains. One had a patch on the seat of his trousers. The other boy made fun of it, and the boy with the patch went home and told his father. Thirty years of local war was the result. The factions fought on after they had forgotten why they had fought at all. While organized warfare is now over, an occasional fight yet comes over the patch on those trousers and a man or two is killed. A county as big as Rhode Island is still bitterly divided on the subject. In a race for the legislature not long ago, the feud was the sole issue. And, without knowing it, perhaps, a mountaineer carried that patch like a flag to victory, and sat under it at the capital—making laws for the rest of the State.

That is the feud that has stained the highland border of the State with blood, and abroad, has engulfed the reputation of the lowland blue-grass, where there are, of course, no feuds—a fact that sometimes seems to require emphasis, I am sorry to say. Almost every mountain county has, or has had, its feud. On one side is a leader whose authority is rarely questioned.

Blue-grass and Rhododendron

Each leader has his band of retainers. Always he arms them; usually he feeds them; sometimes he houses and clothes them, and sometimes, even, he hires them. In one local war, I remember, four dollars per day were the wages of the fighting man, and the leader on one occasion, while besieging his enemies—in the county court-house—tried to purchase a cannon, and from no other place than the State arsenal, and from no other personage than the governor himself.

It is the feud that most sharply differentiates the Kentucky mountaineer from his fellows, and it is extreme isolation that makes possible in this age such a relic of mediæval barbarism. For the feud means, of course, ignorance, shiftlessness, incredible lawlessness, a frightful estimate of the value of human life; the horrible custom of ambush, a class of cowardly assassins who can be hired to do murder for a gun, a mule, or a gallon of moonshine.

Now these are the blackest shadows in the only picture of Kentucky mountain life that has reached the light of print through the press. There is another side, and it is only fair to show it.

The feud is an inheritance. There were feuds before the war, even on the edge of the blue-grass; there were fierce family fights in the backwoods before and during the Revolution—when the war between Whig

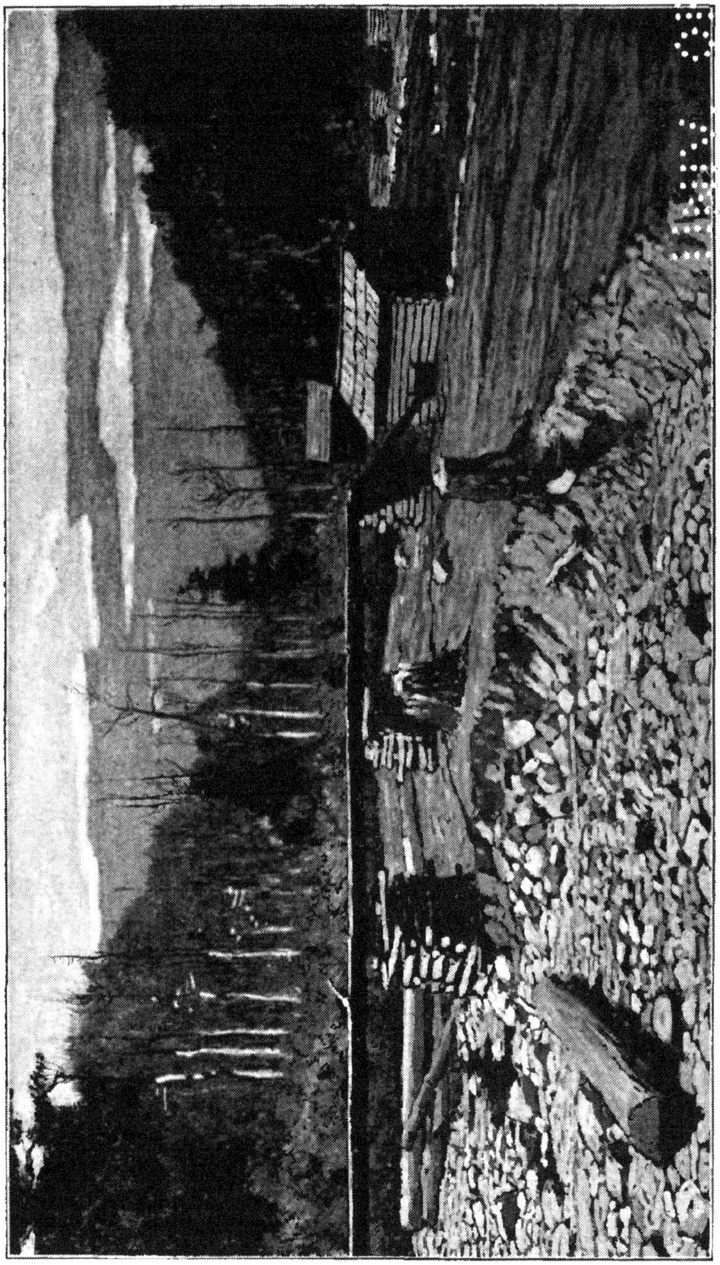

and Tory served as a pretext for satisfying personal animosities already existing, and it is not a wild fancy that the Kentucky mountain feud takes root in Scotland. For, while it is hardly possible that the enmities of the Revolution were transmitted to the Civil War, it is quite sure that whatever race instinct, old-world trait of character, or moral code the backwoodsman may have taken with him into the mountains—it is quite sure that that instinct, that trait of character, that moral code, are living forces in him to-day. The late war was, however, the chief cause of feuds. When it came, the river-bottoms were populated, the clans were formed. There were more slave-holders among them than among other Southern mountaineers. For that reason, the war divided them more evenly against themselves, and set them fighting. When the war stopped elsewhere, it simply kept on with them, because they were more isolated, more evenly divided; because they were a fiercer race, and because the issue had become personal. The little that is going on now goes on for the same reason, for while civilization pressed close enough in 1890 and 1891 to put an end to organized fighting, it is a consistent fact that after the failure of Baring Brothers, and the stoppage of the flow of English capital into the mountains, and the check to railroads and civilization, these feuds slowly started up again. When I left home for the Cuban war, two companies of State militia were on their way to the mountains to put down a feud. On the day of the Las Guasimas fight these feudsmen fought, and they lost precisely as many men killed as the Rough Riders—eight.

Again: while the feud may involve the sympathies of a county, the number of men actually engaged in it are comparatively few. Moreover, the feud is strictly of themselves, and is based primarily on a privilege that the mountaineer, the world over, has most grudgingly surrendered to the law, the privilege of avenging his private wrongs. The non-partisan and the traveller are never molested. Property of the beaten faction is never touched. The women are safe from harm, and I have never heard of one who was subjected to insult. Attend to your own business, side with neither faction in act or word and you are much safer among the Kentucky mountaineers, when a feud is going on, than you are crossing Broadway at Twenty-third Street. As you ride along, a bullet may plough through the road ten yards in front of you. That means for you to halt. A mountaineer will come out of the bushes and ask who you are and where you are going and what your business is. If your answers are satisfactory, you go on unmolested.

The Kentucky Mountaineer

Asking for a place to stay all night, you may be told, "Go to So and So's house; he'll pertect ye;" and he will, too, at the risk of his own life when you are past the line of suspicion and under his roof.

There are other facts that soften a too harsh judgment of the mountaineer and his feud—harsh as the judgment should be. Personal fealty is the cornerstone of the feud. The mountaineer admits no higher law; he understands no conscience that will violate that tie. You are my friend or my kinsman; your quarrel is my quarrel; whoever strikes you, strikes me. If you are in trouble, I must not testify against you. If you are an officer, you must not arrest me, you must send me word to come into court. If I'm innocent, why, maybe I'll come.

Moreover, the worst have the list of rude virtues already mentioned; and, besides, the mountaineer is never a thief nor a robber, and he will lie about one thing and one thing only, and that is land. He has cleared it, built his cabin from the trees, lived on it and he feels that any means necessary to hold it are justifiable. Lastly, religion is as honestly used to cloak deviltry as it ever was in the Middle Ages.

A feud leader who had about exterminated the opposing faction, and had made a good fortune for a mountaineer while doing it, for he kept his men busy getting out timber when they weren't fighting, said to me, in all seriousness:

"I have triumphed agin my enemies time and time agin. The Lord's on my side, and I gits a better and better Christian ever' year."

A preacher, riding down a ravine, came upon an old mountaineer hiding in the bushes with his rifle.

"What are you doing there, my friend?"

"Ride on, stranger," was the easy answer. "I'm a-waitin' fer Jim Johnson, and with the help of the Lawd I'm goin' to blow his damn head off."

Even the ambush, the hideous feature of the feud, took root in the days of the Revolution, and was borrowed, maybe, from the Indians. Milfort, the Frenchman, who hated the backwoodsman, says Mr. Roosevelt, describes with horror their extreme malevolence and their murderous disposition toward one another. He says that whether a wrong had been done to a man personally or to his family, he would, if necessary, travel a hundred miles and lurk around the forest indefinitely to get a chance to shoot his enemy.

But the Civil War was the chief cause of bloodshed; for there is evidence, indeed, that though feeling between families was strong, bloodshed was rare and the

The Kentucky Mountaineer

English sense of fairness prevailed, in certain communities at least. Often you shall hear an old mountaineer say: "Folks usen to talk about how fer they could kill a *deer*. Now hit's how fer they can kill a *man*. Why, I have knowed the time when a man would hev been druv outen the county fer drawin' a knife or a pistol, an' if a man was ever killed, hit wus kinder accidental by a Barlow. I reckon folks got used to weepons an' killin' an' shootin' from the bresh endurin' the war. But hit's been gettin' wuss ever sence, and now hit's dirk an' Winchester all the time." Even for the ambush there is an explanation.

"Oh, I know all the excuses folks make. Hit's fair for one as 'tis fer t'other. You can't fight a man f'ar and squar who'll shoot you in the back. A pore man can't fight money in the courts. Thar hain't no witnesses in the lorrel but leaves, an' dead men don't hev much to say. I know hit all. Looks like lots o' decent young folks hev got usen to the idee; thar's so much of it goin' on and thar's so much talk about shootin' from the bresh. I do reckon hit's wuss'n stealin' to take a feller critter's life that way."

It is also a fact that most of the men who have been engaged in these fights were born, or were children, during the war, and were, in consequence, accustomed to bloodshed and bushwhacking from infancy. Still, even among the fighters there is often a strong prejudice against the ambush, and in most feuds, one or the other side discountenances it, and that is the faction usually defeated. I know of one family that was one by one exterminated because they refused to take to the " bresh."

Again, the secret of the feud is isolation. In the mountains the war kept on longer, for personal hatred supplanted its dead issues. Railroads and newspapers have had their influence elsewhere. Elsewhere court circuits include valley people. Civilization has pressed slowly on the Kentucky mountains. The Kentucky mountaineer, until quite lately, has been tried, when brought to trial at all, by the Kentucky mountaineer. And when a man is tried for a crime by a man who would commit that crime under the same circumstances, punishment is not apt to follow.

Thus the influence that has helped most to break up the feud is trial in the Blue-grass, for there is no ordeal the mountaineer more hates than trial by a jury of bigoted " furriners."

Who they are—these Southern mountaineers—is a subject of endless conjecture and dispute—a question that perhaps will never be satisfactorily solved. While there are among them the descendants of the old bond servant and redemptioner class, of vicious runaway

The Kentucky Mountaineer

criminals and the trashiest of the poor whites, the ruling class has undoubtedly come from the old free settlers, English, German, Swiss, French Huguenot, even Scotch and Scotch-Irish. As the German and Swiss are easily traced to North Carolina, the Huguenots to South Carolina and parts of Georgia, it is more than probable, from the scant study that has been given the question, that the strongest and largest current of blood in their veins comes from none other than the mighty stream of Scotch-Irish.

Briefly, the theory is this: From 1720 to 1780, the settlers in southwest Virginia, middle North Carolina and western South Carolina were chiefly Scotch and Scotch-Irish. They were active in the measures preceding the outbreak of the Revolution, and they declared independence at Abington, Va., even before they did at Mecklenburg, N. C. In these districts they were the largest element in the patriot army, and they were greatly impoverished by the war. Being too poor or too conscientious to own slaves, and unable to compete with them as the planter's field hand, blacksmith, carpenter, wheelwright, and man-of-all-work, especially after the invention of the cotton-gin in 1792, they had no employment and were driven to mountain and sand-hill. There are some good reasons for the theory. Among prominent mountain fami-

Blue-grass and Rhododendron

lies direct testimony or unquestioned tradition point usually to Scotch-Irish ancestry, sometimes to pure Scotch origin, sometimes to English. Scotch-Irish family names in abundance speak for themselves, as do folk-words and folk-songs and the characteristics, mental, moral, and physical, of the people. Broadly speaking, the Southern mountaineers are characterized as "peaceable, civil, good-natured, kind, clever, naturally witty, with a fair share of common-sense, and morals not conscientiously bad, since they do not consider ignorance, idleness, poverty, or the excessive use of tobacco or moonshine as immoral or vicious."

Another student says: "The majority is of good blood, honest, law-abiding blood." Says still another: "They are ignorant of books, but sharp as a rule." Says another: "They have great reverence for the Bible, and are sturdy, loyal, and tenacious." Moreover, the two objections to this theory that would naturally occur to anyone have easy answers. The mountaineers are not Presbyterian and they are not thrifty. Curiously enough, testimony exists to the effect that certain Methodist or Baptist churches were once Presbyterian; and many preachers of these two denominations had grandfathers who were Presbyterian ministers. The Methodists and Baptists were

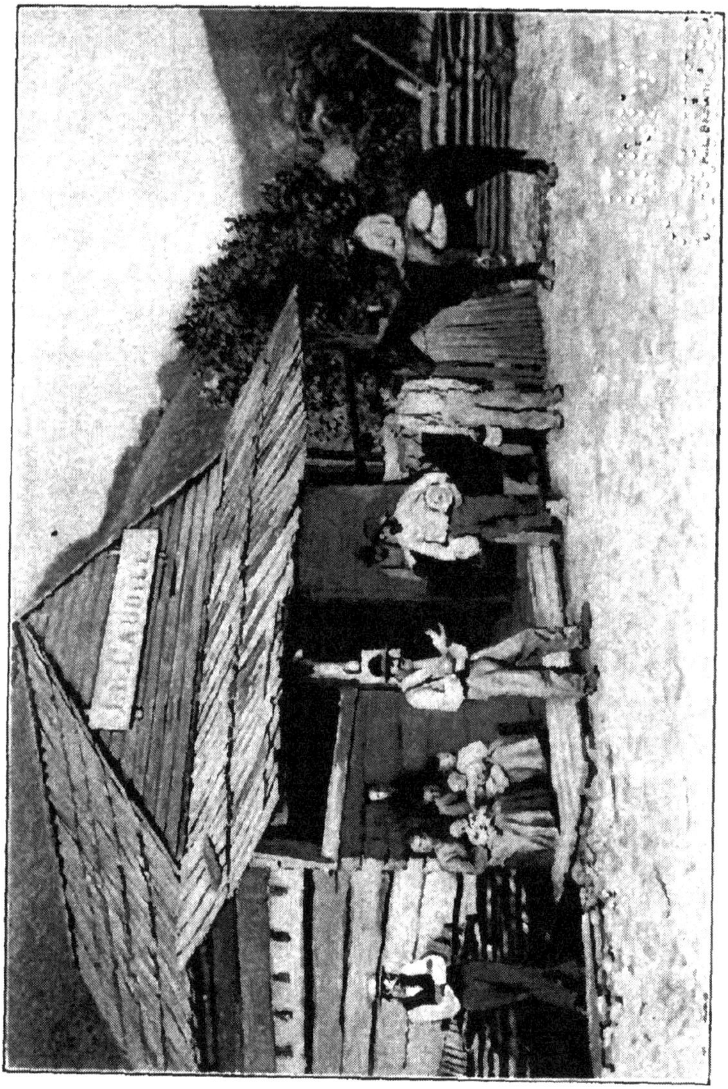

The Kentucky Mountaineer

perhaps more active; they were more popular in the mountains as they were in the backwoods, because they were more democratic and more emotional. The backwoodsman did not like the preacher to be a preacher only. He, too, must work with his hands.

Scotch-Irish thriftiness decayed. The soil was poor; game was abundant; hunting bred idleness. There were no books, no schools, few church privileges, a poorly educated ministry, and the present illiteracy, thriftlessness, and poverty were easy results. Deed-books show that the ancestors of men who now make their mark, often wrote a good hand.

Such, briefly, is the Southern mountaineer in general, and the Kentucky mountaineer in particular. Or, rather, such he was until fifteen years ago, and to know him now you must know him as he was then, for the changes that have been wrought in the last decade affect localities only, and the bulk of the mountain-people is, practically, still what it was one hundred years ago. Still, changes have taken place and changes will take place now swiftly, and it rests largely with the outer world what these changes shall be.

The vanguards of civilization—railroads—unless quickly followed by schools and churches, at the ratio of four schools to one church, have a bad effect on

Blue-grass and Rhododendron

the Southern mountaineer. He catches up the vices of the incoming current only too readily. The fine spirit of his hospitality is worn away. He goes to some little "boom" town, is forced to pay the enormous sum of fifty cents for his dinner, and when you go his way again, you pay fifty cents for yours. Carelessly applied charity weakens his pride, makes him dependent. You hear of arrests for petty thefts sometimes, occasionally burglaries are made, and the mountaineer is cowed by the superior numbers, superior intelligence of the incomer, and he seems to lose his sturdy self-respect.

And yet the result could easily be far different. Not long ago I talked with an intelligent young fellow, a young minister, who had taught among them many years, exclusively in the Kentucky mountains, and is now preaching to them. He says, they are more tractable, more easily moulded, more easily uplifted than the people of a similar grade of intelligence in cities. He gave an instance to illustrate their general susceptibility in all ways. When he took charge of a certain school, every boy and girl, nearly all of them grown, chewed tobacco. The teacher before him used tobacco and even exchanged it with his pupils. He told them at once they must stop. They left off instantly.

The Kentucky Mountaineer

It was a " blab " school, as the mountaineers characterize a school in which the pupils study aloud. He put an end to that in one day, and he soon told them they must stop talking to one another. After school they said they didn't think they could ever do that, but they did. In another county, ten years ago, he had ten boys and girls gathered to organize a Sunday-school. None had ever been to Sunday-school and only two knew what a Sunday-school was. He announced that he would organize one at that place a week later. When he reached the spot the following Sunday, there were seventy-five young mountaineers there. They had sung themselves quite hoarse waiting for him, and he was an hour early. The Sunday-school was founded, built up and developed into a church.

When the first printing-press was taken to a certain mountain-town in 1882, a deputation of citizens met it three miles from town and swore that it should go no farther. An old preacher mounted the wagon and drove it into town. Later the leader of that crowd owned the printing-press and ran it. In this town are two academies for the education of the mountaineer. Young fellows come there from every mountain-county and work their way through. They curry horses, carry water, work about the houses—do everything; many of them cook for themselves and live on four dollars a month. They are quick-witted, strong-minded, sturdy, tenacious, and usually very religious.

Indeed, people who have been among the Southern mountaineers testify that, as a race, they are proud, sensitive, hospitable, kindly, obliging in an unreckoning way that is almost pathetic, honest, loyal, in spite of their common ignorance, poverty, and isolation; that they are naturally capable, eager to learn, easy to uplift. Americans to the core, they make the Southern mountains a store-house of patriotism; in themselves, they are an important offset to the Old World outcasts whom we have welcomed to our shores; and they surely deserve as much consideration from the nation as the negroes, for whom we have done, and are doing so much, or as the heathen, to whom we give millions.

I confess that I have given prominence to the best features of mountain life and character, for the reason that the worst will easily make their own way. It is only fair to add, however, that nothing that has ever been said of the mountaineer's ignorance, shiftlessness, and awful disregard of human life, especially in the Kentucky mountains, that has not its basis, perhaps, in actual fact.

The Kentucky Mountaineer

First, last, and always, however, it is to be remembered that to begin to understand the Southern mountaineers you must go back to the social conditions and standards of the backwoods before the Revolution, for practically they are the backwoods people and the backwoods conditions of pre-Revolutionary days. Many of their ancestors fought with ours for American independence. They were loyal to the Union for one reason that no historian seems ever to have guessed. For the loyalty of 1861 was, in great part, merely the transmitted loyalty of 1776, imprisoned like a fossil in the hills. Precisely for the same reason, the mountaineer's estimate of the value of human life, of the sanctity of the law, of a duty that overrides either —the duty of one blood kinsman to another—is the estimate of that day and not of this; and it is by the standards of that day and not of this that he is to be judged. To understand the mountaineer, then, you must go back to the Revolution. To do him justice you must give him the awful ordeal of a century of isolation and consequent ignorance in which to deteriorate. Do that and your wonder, perhaps, that he is so bad becomes a wonder that he is not worse. To my mind, there is but one strain of American blood that could have stood that ordeal quite so well, and that comes from the sturdy Scotch-Irish who are slowly

Blue-grass and Rhododendron

wresting from Puritan and Cavalier an equal share of the glory that belongs to the three for the part played on the world's stage by this land in the heroic rôle of Liberty.

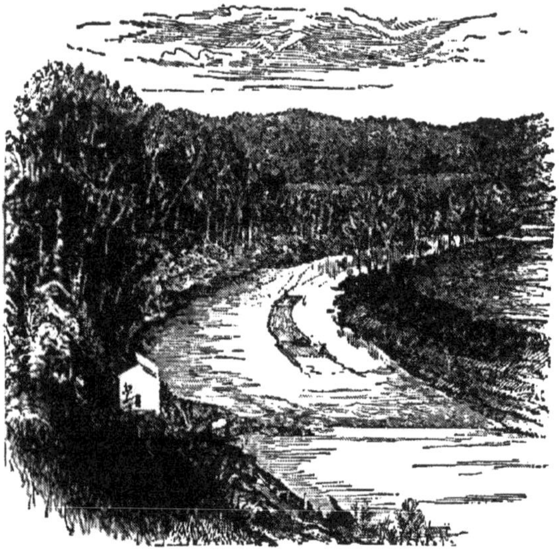

Down the Kentucky on a Raft

THE heart of the Blue-grass in the middle of a sunny afternoon. An hour thence, through a rolling sweep of greening earth and woodland, through the low, poor hills of the brush country and into the oasis of Indian Old Fields, rich in level meadow-lands and wheat-fields. In the good old days of the war-whoop and the scalping-knife, the savage had there one of the only two villages that he ever planted in the "Dark and Bloody Ground." There Daniel Boone camped one night and a pioneer read him "Gulliver's Travels," and the great Daniel called the little stream at their feet Lullibigrub—which name it bears to-day. Another hour between cliffs and pointed peaks and castled rocky summits, and through laurel and rhododendron to the Three Forks of the Kentucky. Up the Middle Fork then and at dusk the end of the railroad in the heart of the mountains and Jackson—the county-seat of "Bloody Breathitt"—once the seat of a lively feud and still the possible seat of another, in spite of the fact that with a manual training-school and a branch of a Blue-grass college, it is also the seat of learning and culture for the region drained by Cutshin, Hell-fer-Sartain, Kingdom Come, and other little streams of a nomenclature not less picturesque. Even Hell-fer-Sartain is looking up. A pious lady has established a Sunday-school on Hell-fer-Sartain. A humorous bookseller has offered to give it a library on the condition that he be allowed to design a book-plate for the volumes. And the Sunday-school is officially known as the "Hell-fer-Sartain Sunday-school." From all these small tributaries of the Kentucky, the mountaineer floats logs down the river to the capital in the Blue-grass. Not many years ago that was his chief reason and his only one for going to the Blue-grass, and down the Kentucky on a raft was the best way for him to get there. He got back on foot. But, coming or going, by steam, water, horseback, or afoot, the trip is well worth while.

At Jackson a man with a lantern put me in a "hack," drove me aboard a flat boat, ferried me over with a rope cable, cracked his whip, and we went up a steep, muddy bank into the town. All through the Cumberland valleys, nowadays, little "boom" towns with electric lights, water-works, and a street-railway make one think of the man who said "give him the

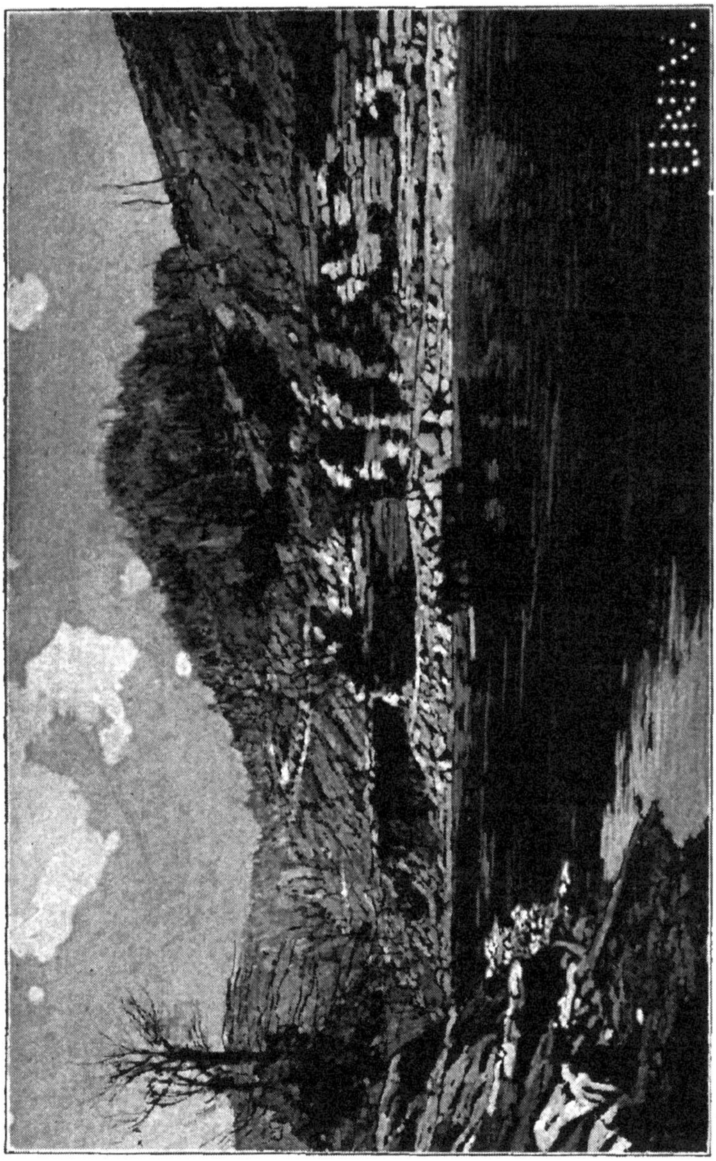

Down the Kentucky on a Raft

luxuries of life and he would do without the necessaries." I did not know that Jackson had ever had a boom, but I thought so when I saw between the flapping curtains of the "hack" what seemed to be a white sidewalk of solid cement.

"Hello," I said, "is that a sidewalk?" The driver grunted, quickly:

"Hit's the side you walk on!"

A wheel of the hack went down to the hub in mud just then and I felt the force of his humor better next morning—I was to get such humor in plenty on the trip—when I went back to the river that same way. It was not a sidewalk of cement but a whitewashed board fence that had looked level in the dark, and except along a muddy foot-wide path close to the fence, passing there, for anything short of a stork on stilts, looked dangerous. I have known mules to drown in a mountain mud-hole.

The "tide," as the mountaineer calls a flood, had come the day before and, as I feared, the rafts were gone. Many of them had passed in the night, and there was nothing to do but to give chase. So I got a row-boat and a mountaineer, and, taking turns at the oars, we sped down the swift yellow water at the clipping rate of ten miles an hour.

As early as the late days of August the mountaineer

Blue-grass and Rhododendron

goes "logging" in order to cut the trees before the sap rises, so that the logs can dry better all winter and float better in the spring. Before frost comes, on river-bank, hill-side, and mountain-top, the cool morning air is resonant with the ring of axes, the singing whistle of big saws, the crash of giant poplar and oak and chestnut down through the lesser growth under them, and the low boom that echoes through the woods when the big trees strike the earth. All winter this goes on. With the hammer of the woodpecker in the early spring, you hear the cries of ox-drivers "snaking" the logs down the mountain-side to the edge of some steep cliff, where they are tumbled pell-mell straight down to the bank of the river, or the bank of some little creek that runs into it. It takes eight yoke of oxen, sometimes, to drag the heart of a monarch to the chute, and there the logs are "rafted" —as the mountaineer calls the work; that is, they are rolled with hand-spikes into the water and lashed side by side with split saplings—lengthwise in the broad Big Sandy, broadside in the narrow Kentucky. Every third or fourth log is a poplar, because that wood is buoyant and will help float the chestnut and the oak. At bow and stern, a huge long limber oar is rigged on a turning stile, the raft is anchored to a tree with a cable of rope or grapevine, and there is a patient wait

Down the Kentucky on a Raft

for a "tide." Some day in March or April—sometimes not until May—mist and clouds loose the rain in torrents, the neighbors gather, the cable is slipped, and the raft swings out the mouth of the creek on its long way to the land of which, to this day, the average mountaineer knows hardly less than that land knows of him.

Steadily that morning we kept the clumsy row-boat sweeping around green-buttressed points and long bends of the river, between high vertical cliffs overspread with vines and streaked white with waterfalls, through boiling eddies and long, swift, waving riffles, in an exhilaration that seems to come to running blood and straining muscles only in lonely wilds. Once a boy shied a stone down at us from the point of a cliff hundreds of feet sheer overhead.

"I wish I had my 44," said the mountaineer, looking wistfully upward.

"You wouldn't shoot at him?"

"I'd skeer him a leetle, I reckon," he said, dryly, and then he told me stories of older and fiercer days when each man carried a "gun," and often had to use it to secure a landing on dark nights when the loggers had to tie up to the bank. When the moon shines, the rafts keep going night and day.

"When the river's purty swift, you know, it's hard

to stop a raft. I've seen a raft slash down through the bushes for two miles before a fellow could git a rope around a tree. So sometimes we had to ketch hold of another feller's raft that was already tied up, and, as there was danger o' pullin' his loose, the feller'd try to keep us off. That's whar the 44's come in. And they do it yit," he said, as, later, I learned for myself.

Here and there were logs and splintered saplings thrown out on the bank of the river—signs of wreckage where a raft had "bowed"; that is, the bow had struck the bank at the bend of the river, the stern had swung around to the other shore, and the raft had hunched up in the middle like a bucking horse. Standing upright, the mountaineer can ride a single log down a swift stream, even when his weight sinks it a foot or two under the surface, but he finds it hard and dangerous to stay aboard a raft when it "bows."

"I was bringin' a raft out o' Leatherwood Creek below heah "—only that was not the name he gave the creek—" and we bowed just before we got to the river. Thar was a kind of a idgit on board who was just a-ridin' down the creek fer fun, and when I was throwed out in the woods I seed him go up in the air and come down kerflop in the water. He went under the raft, and crawled out about two hundred yards

Down the Kentucky on a Raft

down the river. We axed him to git on agin, but that idgit showed more sense than I knowed he had. He said he'd heerd o' hell and high water, and he'd been under one and mighty close to t'other, and he reckoned he'd stay whar he was."

It was getting toward noon now. We had made full forty miles, and Leatherwood was the next stream below.

"We mought ketch a raft thar," said the mountaineer; and we did. Sweeping around the bend I saw a raft two hundred feet long at the mouth of the creek—tugging at its anchor—and a young giant of a mountaineer pushing the bow-oar to and fro through the water to test its suppleness. He had a smile of pure delight on his bearded, winning face when we shot the row-boat alongside.

"I tell you, Jim," he said, "hit's a sweet-pullin' oar."

"It shorely is, Tom," said Jim. "Heah's a furriner that wants to go down the river with ye."

"All right," said the giant, hospitably. "We're goin' just as soon as we can git off."

On the bank was a group of men, women, and children gathered to watch the departure. In a basin of the creek above, men up to their waists in water were "rafting" logs. Higher above was a chute, and down it rolled more logs, jumping from end to end, like jackstraws. Higher, I could hear the hammer of a woodpecker; higher still, the fluting of a wood-thrush, and still higher, an ox-driver's sharp cry. The vivid hues of dress and shawl on the bank seemed to strike out sharply every color-note in the green wall behind them, straight up to the mountain-top. It was as primitive and simple as Arcady.

Down the bank came old Ben Sanders, as I learned later, shouting his good-byes, without looking behind him as he slipped down the bank. Close after him, his son, young Ben, with a huge pone of corn-bread three feet square. The boy was so trembling with excitement over his first trip that he came near dropping it. Then a mountaineer with lank, long hair, the scholar of the party, and Tim, guilty of humor but once on the trip—solemn Tim. Two others jumped aboard with bacon and coffee—passengers like myself. Tom stood on shore with one hand on the cable, while he said something now and then to a girl in crimson homespun who stood near, looking downward. Now and then one of the other women would look at the two and laugh.

"All right now, Tom," shouted old Ben, "let her loose!"

Tom thrust out his hand, which the girl took shyly.

Down the Kentucky on a Raft

"Don't fergit, Tom," she said. Tom laughed—there was little danger that Tom would forget—and with one twist of his sinewy hands he threw the loop of the grapevine clear of the tree and, for all his great bulk, sprang like a cat aboard the raft, which shot forward with such lightness that I was nearly thrown from my feet.

"Good-by, Ben!"

"Good-by, Molly!"

"So long, boys!"

"Don't you fergit that caliker, now, Ben."

"I won't."

"Tom," called a mountaineer, "ef you git drunk an' spend yo' money, Nance heah says she won't marry ye when you come back." Nance slapped at the fellow, and the giant smiled. Then one piping voice:

"Don't fergit my terbacky, Ben."

"All right, Granny—I won't," answered old Ben, and, as we neared the bend of the river, he cried back:

"Take that saddle home I borrowed o' Joe Thomas, an' don't fergit to send that side of bacon to Mandy Longnecker, an'—an'—" and then I got a last glimpse of the women shading their patient eyes to watch the lessening figures on the raft and the creaking oars flashing white in the sunlight; and I thought of them going back to their lonely little cabins on this creek to await the home-coming of the men. If the mountain-women have any curiosity about that distant land, the Blue-grass " settlemints," they never show it. I have never known a mountain-woman to go down the river on a raft. Perhaps they don't care to go; perhaps it is not proper, for their ideas of propriety are very strict; perhaps the long trip back on foot deterred them so long that the habit of not going is too strong to overcome. And then if they did go, who would tend the ever-present baby in arms, the ever-numerous children; make the garden and weed and hoe the young corn for the absent lord and master. I suppose it was generations of just such lonely women, waiting at their cabins in pioneer days for the men to come home, that gives the mountain-woman the brooding look of pathos that so touches the stranger's heart to-day; and it is the watching to-day that will keep unchanged that look of vacant sadness for generations to come.

"Ease her up now!" called old Ben—we were making our first turn—and big Tom at the bow, and young Ben and the scholar at the stern oar, swept the white saplings through the water with a terrific swish. Footholes had been cut along the logs, and in these the men stuck their toes as they pushed, with both hands on the oar and the oar across their breasts. At the end of the stroke, they threw the oar down and up

Down the Kentucky on a Raft

with rhythm and dash. Then they went back on a run to begin another stroke.

"Ease her up—ease her up," said old Ben, soothingly, and then, suddenly:

"Hit her up—hit her up—hell!"

Solemn Tim began to look ashore for a good place to jump. The bow barely slipped past the bend of the river.

"That won't do," said old Ben again; "Hell!" Big Tom looked as crestfallen as a school-boy, and said nothing—we had just escaped "bowing" on our first turn. Ten minutes later we swept into the Narrows—the "Nahrers" as the mountaineer says; and it was quick and dangerous work keeping the unwieldy craft from striking a bowlder, or the solid wall of a vertical cliff that on either side rose straight upward, for the river was pressed into a narrow channel, and ran with terrific force. It was one long exhilarating thrill going through those Narrows, and everybody looked relieved when we slipped out of them into broad water, which ran straight for half a mile—where the oars were left motionless and the men got back their breath and drew their pipes and bottles. I knew the innocent white liquor that revenue man and mountaineer call "moonshine," and a wary sip or two was enough for me. Along with the bottle came the

Blue-grass and Rhododendron

inevitable first question that, under any and all circumstances, every mountaineer asks the stranger, no matter if the stranger has asked him a question first.

"Well, stranger, what mought yo' name be?"

Answering that, you are expected to tell in the same breath, as well, what your business is. I knew it was useless to tell mine—it would not have been understood, and would have engendered suspicion. I was at Jackson; I had long wanted to go down the river on a raft, and I let them think that I was going for curiosity and fun; but I am quite sure they were not wholly satisfied until I had given them ground to believe that I could afford the trip for fun, by taking them up to the hotel that night for supper, and giving them some very bad cigars. For, though the moon was full, the sky was black with clouds, and old Ben said we must tie up for the night. That tying up was exciting work. The raft was worked cautiously toward the shore, and a man stood at bow and stern with a rope, waiting his chance to jump ashore and coil it about a tree. Tom jumped first, and I never realized what the momentum of the raft was until I saw him, as he threw the rope about a tree, jerked like a straw into the bushes, the rope torn from his hands, and heard the raft crashing down through the undergrowth. Tom gave chase along the bank, and

Down the Kentucky on a Raft

everybody yelled and ran to and fro. It was crash—swish—bump—grind and crash again; and it was only by the hardest work at the clumsy oars that we kept the raft off the shore. From a rock Tom made a flying leap aboard again, and luckily the river broadened there, and just past the point of a thicket we came upon another raft already anchored. The boy Ben picked up his rope and prepared to leap aboard the stranger, from the other end of which a mountaineer ran toward us.

"Keep off," he shouted, "keep off, I tell ye," but the boy paid no attention, and the other man pulled his pistol. Ben dropped his rope, then looked around, laughed, picked up his rope again and jumped aboard. The fellow lowered his pistol and swore. I looked around, too, then. Every man on board with us had his pistol in his hand. We tugged the stranger's cable sorely, but it held him fast and he held us fast, and the tying up was done.

"He'd 'a' done us the same way," said old Ben, in palliation.

Next day it was easy sailing most of the time, and we had long rests from the oars, and we smoked, and the bottles were slowly emptied, one by one, while the mountaineers "jollied" each other and told drawling stories. Once we struck a long eddy, and were caught by it and swept back up-stream; twice this happened before we could get in the current again. Then they all laughed and " jollied " old Ben.

It seemed that the old fellow had taken too much one dark night and had refused to tie up. There was a house at the head of this eddy, and when he struck it there was a gray horse hitched to the fence outside; and inside was the sound of fiddles and furious dancing. Next morning old Ben told another raftsman that he had seen more gray horses and heard more fiddling that night than he had seen and heard since he was born.

"They was a-fiddlin' an' a-dancin' at every house I passed last night," he said, " an' I'm damned if I didn't see a gray hoss hitched outside every time I heerd the fiddlin'. I reckon they was ha'nts." The old fellow laughed good-naturedly while the scholar was telling his story. He had been caught in the eddy and had been swung around and around, passing the same house and the same horse each time.

I believe I have remarked that those bottles were emptying fast. By noon they were quite empty, and two hours later, as we rounded a curve, the scholar went to the bow, put his hands to his mouth and shouted:

"Whis-kee!"

Down the Kentucky on a Raft

And again:

"Whiss-kee-ee!"

A girl sprang from the porch of a cabin far down the stream, and a moment later a canoe was pushed from the bushes, and the girl, standing erect, paddled it up-stream close to the bank and shot it out alongside the raft.

"Howdye, Mandy!"

"Howdye, boys!"

Young Ben took two bottles from her, gave her some pieces of silver, and, as we sped on, she turned shoreward again and stood holding the bushes and looking after us, watching young Ben, as he was watching her; for she was black-eyed and pretty.

The sky was broken with hardly a single cloud that night. The moon was yellow as a flame, and we ran all night long. I lay with my feet to the fire that Ben had built on some stones in the middle of the raft, looking up at the trees that arched over us, and the steep, moonlit cliffs, and the moon itself riding high and full and so brilliant that the stars seemed to have fallen in a shower all around the horizon. The raft ran as noiselessly as a lily-pad, and it was all as still and wild as a dream. Once or twice we heard the yelp of a fox-hound and the yell of a hunter out in the hills, and the mountaineers yelled back in answer

Blue-grass and Rhododendron

and hied the dog on. Sometimes young Ben and the scholar, and even solemn Tim, sang some weird old ballad that one can hear now only in the Southern hills; and twice, to my delight and surprise, the scholar "yodelled." I wondered where he had learned how. He did not know—he had always known how. It was perhaps only another of the curious Old World survivals that are of ceaseless interest to a speculative "furriner," and was no stranger than the songs he sang. I went to sleep by and by, and woke up shivering. It was yet dark, but signs of day were evident; and in the dim light I could see young Ben at the stern-oar on watch, and the huge shape of big Tom standing like a statue at the bow and peering ahead. We had made good time during the night—the mountaineers say a raft makes better time during the night —why, I could not see, nor could they explain, and at daybreak we were sweeping around the hills of the brush country, and the scholar who had pointed out things of interest (he was a school-teacher at home) began to show his parts with some pride. Every rock and cliff and turn and eddy down that long river has some picturesque name that the river-men have given it—names known only to them. Two rocks that shoved their black shoulders up on either side of the stream have been called Buck and Billy, after some

Down the Kentucky on a Raft

old fellow's favorite oxen, for more than half a century. Here was an eagle's nest. A bear had been seen not long ago, looking from a black hole in the face of a cliff. How he got there no one could understand. The scholar told some strong stories—now that we were in a region of historical interest—where Boone planted his first fort and where Boonesborough once stood, but he always prefaced his tale with the overwhelming authority that—

"Hist'ry says!"

He declared that history said that a bull, seeing some cows across the river, had jumped from the point of a high cliff straight down into the river; had swum across and fallen dead as he was climbing the bank.

"He busted his heart," said the scholar.

Oddly enough, solemn Tim, who had never cracked a smile, was the first to rebel.

"You see that cliff yander?" said the scholar. "Well, hist'ry says that Dan'l Boone druv three Injuns once straight over that cliff down into the river."

I could see that Tim was loath to cast discredit on the facts of history. If the scholar had said one or even two Indians, I don't think Tim would have called a halt; but for Daniel, with only one load in his gun

Blue-grass and Rhododendron

—and it not a Winchester—to drive *three*—it was too much. And yet Tim never smiled, and it was the first time I heard him voluntarily open his lips.

"Well, hist'ry mought 'a' said that," he said, "but I reckon *Dan'l was in the lead!*" The yell that went up routed the scholar and stilled him. History said no farther down that stream, even when we were passing between the majestic cliffs that in one place are spanned by the third highest bridge in the world. There a ferry was crossing the river, and old Ben grew reminiscential. He had been a ferryman back in the mountains.

"Thar was a slosh of ice runnin' in the river," he said, "an' a feller come a-lopin' down the road one day, an' hollered an' axed me to take him across. I knowed from his voice that he was a-drinkin', and I hollered back an' axed him if he was drunk.

"'Yes, I'm drunk!'

"'How drunk?' I says.

"'Drunk as hell!' he says, 'but I can ride that boat.'

"Well, there was a awful slosh o' ice a-runnin', but I let him on, an' we hadn't got more'n ten feet from the bank when that feller fell off in that slosh o' ice. Well, I ketched him by one foot, and I drug him an' I drug him an' I drug his face about twenty feet in

Down the Kentucky on a Raft

the mud, an' do you know that damn fool come might' nigh a-drownin' before I could *change eends!*"

Thence on, the trip was monotonous except for the Kentuckian who loves every blade of grass in his land —for we struck locks and dams and smooth and slower water, and the hills were low but high enough to shut off the blue-grass fields. But we knew they were there—slope and woodland, bursting into green—and the trip from highland to lowland, barren hillside to rich pasture-land—from rhododendron to blue-grass —was done.

At dusk that day we ran slowly into the little Kentucky capital, past distilleries and brick factories with tall smoking stacks and under the big bridge and, wonder of wonders to Ben, past a little stern-wheel steamboat wheezing up-stream. We climbed the bank into the town, where the boy Ben and solemn Tim were for walking single file in the middle of the streets until called by the scholar to the sidewalk. The boy's eyes grew big with wonder when he saw streets and houses of stone, and heard the whistles of factories and saw what was to him a crush of people in the sleepy little town. I parted from them that night, but next morning I saw big Tom passing the station on foot. He said his companions had taken his things and gone on by train, and that he was

Blue-grass and Rhododendron

going to walk back. I wondered, and while I asked no questions, I should like to wager that I guessed the truth. Tom had spent every cent of his money for the girl in crimson homespun who was waiting for him away back in the hills, and if I read her face aright I could have told him that she would have given every trinket he had sent her rather than wait a day longer for the sight of his face. We shook hands, and I watched him pass out of sight with his face set homeward across and beyond the blue-grass, through the brush country and the Indian Old Fields, back to his hills of laurel and rhododendron.

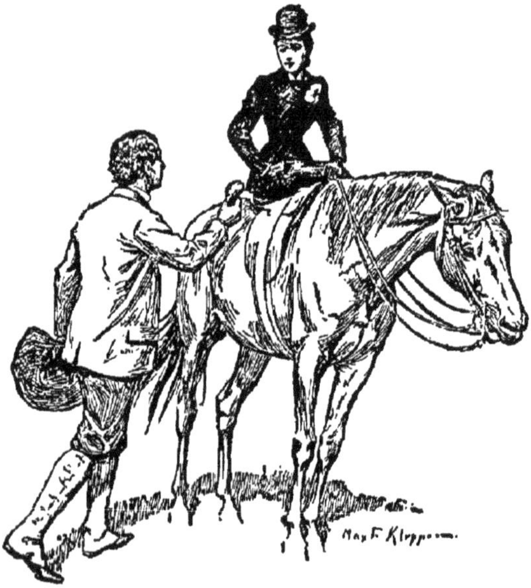
Max F. Klepper

After Br'er Rabbit in the Blue-grass

FOR little more than a month Jack Frost has been busy—that arch-imp of Satan who has got himself enshrined in the hearts of little children. After the clear sunset of some late October day, when the clouds have hung low and kept the air chill, he has a good night for his evil work. By dawn the little magician has spun a robe of pure white, and drawn it close to the breast of the earth. The first light turns it silver, and shows the flowers and jewels with which wily Jack has decked it, so that it may be mistaken for a wedding-gown, perhaps, instead of a winding-sheet. The sun, knowing better, lifts, lets loose his tiny warriors, and, from pure love of beauty, with one stroke smites it gold. Then begins a battle which ends soon in crocodile tears of reconciliation from dauntless little Jack, with the blades of grass and the leaves in their scarlet finery sparkling with the joy of another day's deliverance, and the fields grown gray and aged in a single night. On just such a morning, and before the fight is quite done, saddle-

Blue-grass and Rhododendron

horses are stepping from big white barns in certain counties of the Blue-grass, and, sniffing the cool air, are being led to old-fashioned stiles, from which a little later they bear master or mistress out to the turnpike and past flashing fields to the little county-seat several miles away. There in the court-house square they gather, the gentlefolk of country and town, and from that point they start into the country the other way. It is a hunting-meet. Br'er Rabbit is the quarry, and they are going for him on horseback without dog, stick, snare, or gun—a unique sport, and, so far as I know, confined wholly to the Blue-grass. There is less rusticity than cosmopolitanism in that happy land. The townspeople have farms, and the farmers own stores; intercourse between town and country is unrestrained; and as for social position, that is a question one rarely hears discussed: one either has it unquestioned, or one has it not at all. So out they go, the hunters on horseback, and the chaperons and spectators in buggies, phaetons, and rockaways, through a morning that is cloudless and brilliant, past fields that are sober with autumn, and woods that are dingy with oaks and streaked with the fire of sumac and maple. New hemp lies in shining swaths on each side, while bales of last year's crop are going to market along the white turnpike. Already the farmers

After Br'er Rabbit

are turning over the soil for the autumn sowing of wheat. Corn-shucking is just over, and ragged darkies are straggling from the fields back to town. Through such a scene move horse and vehicle, the riders shouting, laughing, running races, and a quartet, perhaps, in a rockaway singing some old-fashioned song full of tune and sentiment. Six miles out, they turn in at a gate, where a big square brick house with a Grecian portico stands far back in a wooded yard, with a fish-pond on one side and a great smooth lawn on the other. Other hunters are waiting there, and the start is made through a Blue-grass woodland, greening with a second spring, and into a sweep of stubble and ragweed. There are two captains of the hunt. One is something of a wag, and has the voice of a trumpet.

"Form a line, and form a good un!" he yells, and the line stretches out with a space of ten or fifteen feet between each horse and his neighbor on each side. The men are dressed as they please, the ladies as they please. English blood gets expression, as usual, in independence absolute. There is a sturdy disregard of all considerations of form. Some men wear leggings, some high boots; a few have brown shooting-coats. Most of them ride with the heel low and the toes turned, according to temperament. The Southern

Blue-grass and Rhododendron

woman's long riding-skirt has happily been laid aside. These young Dianas wear the usual habit; only the hat is a derby, a cap, sometimes a beaver with a white veil, or a tam-o'-shanter that has slipped down behind and left a frank bare head of shining hair. They hold the reins in either hand, and not a crop is to be seen. There are plenty of riding-whips, however, and sometimes one runs up the back of some girl's right arm, for that is the old-fashioned position for the whip when riding in form. On a trip like this, however, everybody rides to please his fancy, and rides anywhere but off his horse. The men are sturdy country youths, who in a few years will make good types of the beef-eating young English squire—sunburned fellows with big frames, open faces, fearless eyes, and a manner that is easy, cordial, kindly, independent. The girls are midway between the types of brunette and blonde, with a leaning toward the latter type. The extreme brunette is as rare as is the unlovely blonde, whom Oliver Wendell Holmes differentiates from her dazzling sister with locks that have caught the light of the sun. Radiant with freshness these girls are, and with good health and strength; round of figure, clear of eye and skin, spirited, soft of voice, and slow of speech.

There is one man on a sorrel mule. He is the host back at the big farm-house, and he has given up every

After Br'er Rabbit

horse he has to guests. One of the girls has a broad white girth running all the way around both horse and saddle. Her habit is the most stylish in the field; she has lived a year in Washington, perhaps, and has had a finishing touch at a fashionable school in New York. Near her is a young fellow on a black thoroughbred —a graduate, perhaps, of Yale or Princeton. They rarely put on airs, couples like these, when they come back home, but drop quietly into their old places with friends and kindred. From respect to local prejudice, which has a hearty contempt for anything that is not carried for actual use, she has left her riding-crop at home. He has let his crinkled black hair grow rather long, and has covered it with a black slouch-hat. Contact with the outer world has made a difference, however, and it is enough to create a strong bond of sympathy between these two, and to cause trouble between country-bred Phyllis, plump, dark-eyed, bare-headed, who rides a pony that is trained to the hunt, as many of the horses are, and young farmer Corydon, who is near her on an iron-gray. Indeed, mischief is brewing among those four. At a brisk walk the line moves across the field, the captain at each end yelling to the men—only the men, for no woman is ever anywhere but where she ought to be in a Southern hunting-field —to keep it straight.

Blue-grass and Rhododendron

"Billy," shouts the captain with the mighty voice, "I fine you ten dollars." The slouch-hat and the white girth are lagging behind. It is a lovers' quarrel, and the girl looks a little flushed, while Phyllis watches smiling. "But you can compromise with me," adds the captain, and a jolly laugh runs down the line. Now comes a "rebel yell." Somewhere along the line, a horse leaps forward. Other horses jump too; everybody yells, and everybody's eye is on a little bunch of cotton that is being whisked with astonishing speed through the brown weeds. There is a massing of horses close behind it; the white girth flashes in the midst of the mêlée, and the slouch-hat is just behind. The bunch of cotton turns suddenly, and doubles back between the horses' feet. There is a great crash, and much turning, twisting, and sawing of bits. Then the crowd dashes the other way, with Corydon and Phyllis in the lead. The fun has begun.

II

FROM snow to snow in the Blue-grass, Br'er Rabbit has two inveterate enemies—the darky and the schoolboy—and his lot is a hard one. Even in the late spring and early summer, when "ole Mis'" Rabbit is keeping house, either one of her foes will cast a de-

After Br'er Rabbit

structive stone at her, if she venture into open lane or pasture. When midsummer comes even, her tiny, long-eared brood is in danger. Not one of the little fellows is much larger than your doubled fist when the weeds get thick and high, and the elderberries are ripe, and the blackberries almost gone, but he is a tender morsel, and, with the darky, ranks in gastronomical favor close after the 'possum and the coon. You see him then hopping about the edge of hemp and harvest fields, or crossing the country lanes, and he is very pretty, and so innocent and unwary that few have the heart to slay him, except his two ruthless foes. When the fields of grain are cut at harvest-time, both are on a close lookout for him. For, as the grain is mown about him, he is penned at last in a little square of uncut cover, and must make a dash for liberty through stones, sticks, dogs, and yelling darkies. After frost comes, the school-boy has both eyes open for him, and a stone ready, on his way to and from his books, and he goes after him at noon recess and on Saturdays. The darky travels with a " rabbit-stick " three feet long in hand and a cur at his heels. Sometimes he will get his young master's bird-dog out, and give Br'er Rabbit a chase, in spite of the swearing that surely awaits him, and the licking that may. Then he makes a " dead fall " for him—a broad board sup-

Blue-grass and Rhododendron

porting a heavy rock, and supported by triggers that are set like the lines of the figure 4; or he will bend the top of a young sapling to the ground, and make a snare of a string, and some morning there is innocent Br'er Rabbit strung up like a murderer. Sometimes he will chase him into a rock fence, and then what is a square yard or so of masonry to one fat rabbit? Sometimes Br'er Rabbit will take a favorite refuge, a hollow tree; for, while he cannot climb a tree in the usual way, he can arch his back and rise spryly enough on the inside. Then does the ingenious darky contrive a simple instrument of torture—a long, limber stick with a prong, or a split end. This he twists into Br'er Rabbit's fur until he can gather up with it one fold of his slack hide, and down comes the game. This hurts, and with this provocation only will the rabbit snap at the hunter's hand. If this device fails the hunter, he will try smoking him out; and if that fails, there is left the ax. Always, too, is the superstitious darky keen for the rabbit that is caught in a graveyard, by a slow hound, at midnight, and in the dark of the moon. The left hind foot of that rabbit is a thing to conjure with.

On Saturdays, both his foes are after him with dog and gun. If they have no dog they track him in the snow, or they " look for him settin' " in thick bunches

After Br'er Rabbit

of winter blue-grass, or under briers and cut thorn-bushes that have been piled in little gullies; and, alas! they "shoot him settin'" until the darky has learned fair play from association, or the boy has had it thumped into him at school. Then will the latter give Br'er Rabbit a chance for his life by stirring him up with his brass-toed boot and taking a crack at him as he lopes away. It will be a long time before this boy will get old enough, or merciful enough to resist the impulse to get out of his buggy or off his horse, no matter where he is going or in how great a hurry, and shy a stone when a cottontail crosses his path. Indeed, a story comes down that a field of slaves threw aside their hoes once and dashed pell-mell after a passing rabbit. An indignant observer reported the fact to their master, and this was the satisfaction he got.

"Run him, did they?" said the master, cheerfully. "Well, I'd have whipped the last one of them, if they hadn't."

And yet it is not until late in October that Br'er Rabbit need go into the jimson-weeds and seriously "wuck he haid" (work his head) over his personal safety; but it is very necessary then, and on Thanksgiving Day it behooves him to say his prayers in the thickest cover he can find. Every man's hand is against him that day. All the big hunting-parties are out, and the Iroquois Club of Lexington goes for him with horse and greyhound. And that is wild sport. Indeed, put a daredevil Kentuckian on a horse or behind him, and in a proper mood, and there is always wild sport—for the onlooker as well. It is hard to fathom the spirit of recklessness that most sharply differentiates the Southern hunter from his Northern brother, and that runs him amuck when he comes into contact with a horse, whether riding, driving, or betting on him. If a thing has to be done in a hunting-field, or can be done, there is little difference between the two. Only the thing must, with the Northerner, be a matter of skill and judgment, and he likes to know his horse. To him, or to an Englishman, the Southern hunter's performances on a green horse look little short of criminal. In certain counties of Virginia, where hunters follow the hounds after the English fashion, the main point seems to be for each man to "hang up" the man behind him, and desperate risks are run. "I have stopped that boyish foolishness, though," said an aged hunter under thirty; "I give my horse a chance." In other words, he had stopped exacting of him the impossible. In Georgia, they follow hounds at a fast gallop through wooded bogs and swamps at night, and I have seen a horse go down twice within a distance of thirty yards, and

After Br'er Rabbit

the rider never leave his back. The same is true of Kentucky, and I suppose of other Southern States. I have known one of my friends in the Blue-grass to amuse himself by getting into his buggy an unsuspecting friend, who was as sedate then as he is now (and he is a judge now), and driving him at full speed through an open gate, then whizzing through the woods and seeing how near he could graze the trunks of trees in his course, and how sharply he could turn, and ending up the circuit by dashing, still at full speed, into a creek, his companion still sedate and fearless, but swearing helplessly. Being bantered by an equally reckless friend one dark midnight while going home, this same man threw both reins out on his horse's back, and gave the high-strung beast a smart cut with his whip. He ran four miles, kept the pike by some mercy of Providence, and stopped exhausted at his master's gate.

A Northern visitor was irritated by the apparently reckless driving of his host, who is a famous horseman in the Blue-grass.

"You lunatic," he said, "you'd better drive over those stone piles!" meaning a heap of unbroken rocks that lay on one side of the turnpike.

"I will," was the grave answer, and he did.

This is the Kentuckian in a buggy.

Blue-grass and Rhododendron

Imagine him on horseback, with no ladies present to check the spirit or the spirits of the occasion, and we can believe that the Thanksgiving hunt of the Iroquois Club is perhaps a little more serious business than playing polo, or riding after anise-seed. And yet there is hardly a member of this club who could sit in his saddle over the course at Meadowbrook or Chevy Chase, for the reason that he has never practised jumping a horse in his stride, and because when he goes fast he takes the jockey seat, which is not, I believe, a good seat for a five-foot fence; at the same time, there is hardly a country-bred rider in the Blue-grass, man or woman, who would not try it. Still, accidents are rare, and it is yet a tenet in the creed of the Southern hunter that the safer plan is to take no care. On the chase with greyhounds the dogs run, of course, by sight, and the point with the huntsman is to be the first at the place of the kill. As the greyhound tosses the rabbit several feet in the air and catches it when it falls, the place is seen by all, and there is a mad rush for that one spot. The hunters crash together, and often knock one another down. I have known two fallen horses and their riders to be cleared in a leap by two hunters who were close behind them. One of the men was struck by a hoof flying over him.

After Br'er Rabbit

"I saw a shoe glisten," he said, "and then it was darkness for a while."

But it is the hunting without even a dog that is interesting, because it is unique and because the ladies share the fun. The sport doubtless originated with school-boys. They could not take dogs, or guns, to school; they had leisure at "big recess," as the noon hour was called; they had horses, and the rabbits were just over the school-yard fence. One day two or three of them chased a rabbit down, and the fun was discovered. These same boys, perhaps, kept up the hunt after their school-days were over, and gave the fever to others, the more easily as foxes began to get scarce. Then the ladies began to take part, and the sport is what it is to-day. The President signs a great annual death-warrant for Br'er Rabbit in the Bluegrass when he fixes a day for Thanksgiving.

III

AGAIN Br'er Rabbit twists, and Phyllis's little horse turns after him like a polo pony after a ball. The black thoroughbred makes a wide sweep; Corydon's iron-gray cuts in behind, and the whole crowd starts in a body toward the road. This rabbit is an old hand at this business, and he knows where safety lies. A

Blue-grass and Rhododendron

moment later the horses come to their haunches at the pike fence. Br'er Rabbit has gone into a culvert under the road, and already a small boy and a yellow dog are making for that culvert from a farm-house near. Again the trumpet, "Form a line!" Again the long line starts. There has been a shifting of positions. Corydon is next the white girth and stylish habit now, and he looks very much pleased. The slouch-hat of the college man and Phyllis's bare head are together, and the thoroughbred's master is talking earnestly. Phyllis looks across the field and smiles. Silly Corydon! The slouch-hat is confessing his trouble to Phyllis and asking advice. Yes, she will help, as women will, out of pure friendship, pure unselfishness; sometimes they have other reasons, and Phyllis had two. Another yell, another rabbit. Off they go, and then, midway, still another cry and still another rabbit. The hunters part in twain, the black thoroughbred leading one wing, the iron-gray the other. Watch the slouch-hat now, and you shall see how the thing is done. The thoroughbred is learning what his master is after, and he swerves to the right; others are coming in from that direction; the rabbit must turn again; others that way, too. Poor Mollie is confused; whichever way her big, startled eyes turn, that way she sees a huge beast and a yelling demon bearing down on

After Br'er Rabbit

her. The slouch-hat swoops near her first, flings himself from his horse, and, in spite of the riders pressing in on him, is after her on foot. Two others swing from their horses on the other side. Mollie makes several helpless hops, and the three scramble for her. The riders in front cry for those behind to hold their horses back, but they crowd in, and it is a miracle that none of the three is trampled down. The rabbit is hemmed in now; there is no way of escape, and instinctively she shrinks frightened to the earth. That is the crucial instant; down goes her pursuer on top of her as though she were a football, and the quarry is his. One blow of the hand behind the long ears, or one jerk by the hind legs, which snaps the neck as a whip cracks, and the slouch-hat holds aloft the brush, a little puff of down, and turns his eye about the field. The white girth is near, and as he starts toward her he is stopped by a low " Ahem! " behind him. Corydon has caught the first rabbit, and already on the derby hat above the white girth is pinned the brush. The young fellow turns again. Phyllis, demure and unregarding, is there with her eyes on the horns of her saddle; but he understands, and a moment later she smiles with prettily feigned surprise, and the white puff moves off in her loosening brown hair. The white girth is betrayed into the faintest shadow of vexation. Corydon heard that eloquent little clearing of the throat with a darkling face, and, indeed, no one of the four looks very happy, except Phyllis.

"Form a line!"

Again the rabbits jump—one, two, three—and the horses dash and crash together, and the men swing to the ground, and are pushed and trampled in a mad clutch for Mollie's long ears; for it is a contest between them as to who shall catch the most game. The iron-gray goes like a demon, and when Corydon drops, the horse is trained to stop and to stand still. This gives Corydon an advantage which balances the superior quickness of the thoroughbred and the agility of his rider. The hunting-party is broken up now into groups of three and four, each group after a rabbit, and, for the time, the disgusted captains give up all hope of discipline. A horse has gone down in a gully. Two excited girls have jumped to the ground for a rabbit. The big mule threshes the weeds like a tornado. Crossing the field at a heavy gallop, he stops suddenly at a ditch, the girth of the old saddle breaks, and the host of the day goes on over the long ears. When he rises from the weeds, there is a shriek of laughter over the field, and then a mule-race, for, with a bray of freedom, the sorrel makes for home. Not a rabbit is jumped on the next circuit; that field

Down goes her pursuer on top of her.

After Br'er Rabbit

is hunted out. No matter; there is another just across the meadow, and they make for it. More than a dozen rabbits dangle head downward behind the saddles of the men. Corydon has caught seven, and the slouch-hat five. The palm lies between them plainly, as does a bigger motive than the game. It is a matter of gallantry—conferring the brush in the field; indeed, secrets are hidden rather than betrayed in that way: so Corydon is free to honor the white girth, and the slouch-hat can honor Phyllis without suspicion. The stylish habit shows four puffs of down; Phyllis wears five—every trophy that the slouch-hat has won. That is the way Phyllis is helping a friend, getting even with an enemy, and putting down a rebellion in her own camp. Even in the meadow a rabbit starts up, and there is a quick sprint in the open; but Br'er Rabbit, another old hand at the hunt, slips through the tall palings of a garden fence. In the other field the fun is more furious than ever, for the rabbits are thicker and the rivalry is very close. Corydon is getting excited; once, he nearly overrides his rival.

The field has gone mad. The girl with the white girth is getting flushed with something more than excitement, and even Phyllis, demure as she still looks, is stirred a little. The pony's mistress is ahead by two brushes, and the white girth is a little vexed. She declares she is going to catch a rabbit herself. The slouch-hat hears, and watches her, thereafter, uneasily. And she does spring lightly, recklessly, to the ground just as the iron-gray and the thoroughbred crash in toward her, and, right between the horses' hoofs, Br'er Rabbit is caught in her little black riding-gloves. Indeed, the front feet of a horse strike her riding-skirt, mashing it into the soft earth, and miss crushing her by a foot. The slouch-hat is on the ground beside her. "You mustn't do that again!" he says with sharp authority.

"Mr. ——," she says, quietly, but haughtily, to Corydon, who is on the ground, too, "will you please help me on my horse?"

The slouch-hat looks as red as a flame, but Phyllis whispers comfort. "That's all right," she says, wisely; and it is all right. Under the slouch-hat, the white face meant fear, anxiety, distress. The authority of the voice thrilled the girl, and in the depths of her heart she was pleased, and Phyllis knew.

The sun is dropping fast, but they will try one more field, which lies beyond a broad pasture of blue-grass. Now comes the chase of the day. Something big and gray leaps from a bunch of grass and bounds away. It is the father of rabbits, and there is a race indeed —an open field, a straight course, and no favor. The

After Br'er Rabbit

devil take the hindmost! Listen to the music of the springy turf, and watch that thoroughbred whose master has stayed behind to put up the fence! He hasn't had half a chance before. He feels the grip of knees as his master rises to the racing-seat, and knowing what that means, he lengthens. No great effort is apparent; he simply stretches himself close to the earth and skims it as a swallow skims a pond. Within two hundred yards he is side by side with Corydon, who is leading, and Corydon, being no fool, pulls in and lets him go on. Br'er Rabbit is going up one side of a long, shallow ravine. There is a grove of locusts at the upper end. The hunters behind see the slouch-hat cut around the crest of the hill, and, as luck would have it, Br'er Rabbit doubles, and comes back on the other side of the ravine. The thoroughbred has closed up the gap that the turn made, and is not fifty yards behind. Br'er Rabbit is making either for a rain-washed gully just opposite, or for a brier-patch farther down. So they wait. The cottontail clears the gully like a ball of thistledown, and Phyllis hears a little gasp behind her as the thoroughbred, too, rises and cleaves the air. Horse and rabbit dash into the weedy cover, and the slouch-hat drops out of sight as three hunters ride yelling into it from the other side. There is a scramble in the bushes, and the slouch-hat

Blue-grass and Rhododendron

emerges with the rabbit in his hand. As he rides slowly toward the waiting party, he looks at Phyllis as though to receive further orders. He gets them. Wily Phyllis shakes her head as though to say:

"Not me this time; *her*."

And with a courtly inclination of the slouch-hat, the big brush goes to the white girth, in lieu of an olive-branch, for peace.

The shadows are stretching fast; they will not try the other field. Back they start through the radiant air homeward, laughing, talking, bantering, living over the incidents of the day, the men with one leg swung over the pommel of their saddles for rest; the girls with habits disordered and torn, hair down, and a little tired, but all flushed, clear-eyed, and happy. The leaves, russet, gold, and crimson, are dropping to the green earth; the sunlight is as yellow as the wings of a butterfly; and on the horizon is a faint haze that foreshadows the coming Indian summer. If it be Thanksgiving, a big dinner will be waiting for them at the stately old farm-house, or if a little later in the year, a hot supper instead. If the hunt is very informal, and there be neither, which rarely happens, everybody asks everybody else to go home with him, and everybody means it, and accepts if possible. This time it is warm enough for a great spread out in the

After Br'er Rabbit

yard on the lawn and under the big oaks. What a feast that is—chicken, turkey, cold ham, pickles, croquettes, creams, jellies, " beaten " biscuit! And what happy laughter, and thoughtful courtesy, and mellow kindness!

Inside, most likely, it is cool enough for a fire in the big fireplace with the shining old brass andirons; and what quiet, solid, old-fashioned English comfort that light brings out! Two darky fiddlers are waiting on the back porch—waiting for a dram from "young cap'n," as "young marster" is now called. They do not wait long. By the time darkness settles, the fiddles are talking old tunes, and the nimble feet are busy. Like draws to like now, and the window-seats and the tall columns of the porch hear again what they have been listening to for so long. Corydon has drawn near. Does Phyllis sulk or look cold? Not Phyllis. You would not know that Corydon had ever left her side. It has been a day of sweet mischief to Phyllis.

At midnight they ride forth in pairs into the crisp, brilliant air and under the kindly moon. The white girth turns toward town with the thoroughbred at her side, and Corydon and Phyllis take the other way. They live on adjoining farms, these two. Phyllis has not forgotten; oh, no! There is mild torture await-

Blue-grass and Rhododendron

ing Corydon long after he shall have forgotten the day, and he deserves it. Silly Corydon! to quarrel over nothing, and to think that he could make her jealous over that—the white girth is never phrased, for Phyllis stops there. It is not the first time these two girls have crossed foils. But there is peace now, and the little comedy of the day, seen by nearly every woman and by hardly a man, comes that night to a happy end.

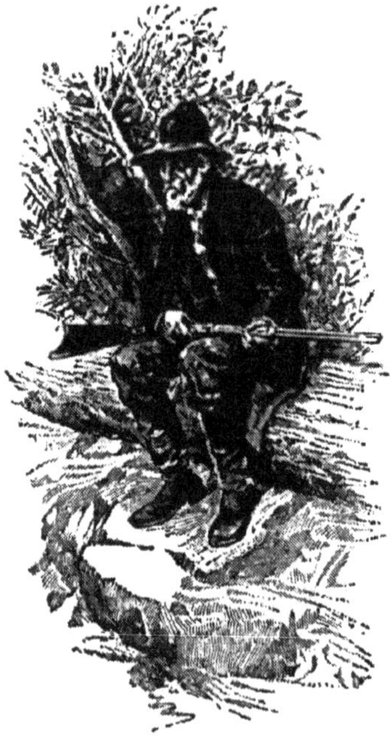

Through the Bad Bend

A WILDLY beautiful cleft through the Cumberland Range opens into the head of Powell's Valley, in Virginia, and forms the Gap. From this point a party of us were going bass-fishing on a fork of the Cumberland River over in the Kentucky mountains. It was Sunday, and several Kentucky mountaineers had crossed over that day to take their first ride on the cars, and to see " the city " —as the Gap has been prophetically called ever since it had a cross-roads store, one little hotel, two farmhouses, and a blacksmith's shop. From them we learned that we could ride down Powell's Valley and get to the fork of the Cumberland by simply climbing over the mountain. As the mountaineers were going back home the same day, Breck and I boarded the train with them, intending to fish down the fork of the river to the point where the rest of the party would strike the same stream, two days later.

At the second station down the road a crowd of Virginia mountaineers got on board. Most of them had been drinking, and the festivities soon began. One drunken young giant pulled his revolver, swung it back over his shoulder—the muzzle almost grazing a woman's face behind him—and swung it up again to send a bullet crashing through the top of the car. The hammer was at the turning-point when a companion caught his wrist. At the same time, the fellow's sister sprang across the aisle, and, wrenching the weapon from his grasp, hid it in her dress. Simultaneously his partner at the other end of the car was drawing a .45 Colt's half as long as his arm. A quick panic ran through the car, and in a moment there was no one in it with us but the mountaineers, the conductor, one brakeman, and one other man, who sat still in his seat, with one hand under his coat. The prospect was neither pleasant nor peaceful, and we rose to our feet and waited. The disarmed giant was raging through the aisle searching and calling, with mighty oaths, for his pistol. The other had backed into a corner of the car, waving his revolver, turning his head from side to side to avoid a surprise in the rear, white with rage, and just drunk enough to shoot. The little conductor was unmoved and smiling, and, by some quiet mesmerism, he kept the two in subjection until the station was reached.

The train moved out and left us among the drunken

Through the Bad Bend

maniacs, no house in sight, the darkness settling on us, and the unclimbed mountain looming up into it. The belligerents paid no attention to us, however, but disappeared quickly, with an occasional pistol-shot and a yell from the bushes, each time sounding farther away. The Kentucky mountaineers were going to climb the mountain. A storm was coming, but there was nothing else to do. So we shouldered our traps and followed them.

There were eight of us—an old man and his two daughters, the husband of one of these, the sweetheart of the other, and a third man, who showed suspicion of us from the beginning. This man with a flaring torch led the way; the old man followed him, and there were two mountaineers deep between the girls and us, who went last.

It was not long before a ragged line of fire cut through the blackness overhead, and the thunder began to crash and the rain to fall. The torch was beaten out, and for a moment there was a halt. Breck and I could hear a muffled argument going on in the air above us, and, climbing toward the voices, we felt the lintel of a mountain-cabin and heard a long drawl of welcome.

The cabin was one dark room without even a loft, the home of a newly married pair. They themselves

Blue-grass and Rhododendron

had evidently just gotten home, for the hostess was on her knees at the big fireplace, blowing a few coals into a blaze. The rest of us sat on the two beds in the room waiting for the fire-light, and somebody began talking about the trouble on the train.

"Did you see that feller settin' thar with his hand under his coat while Jim was tryin' to shoot the brakeman?" said one. "Well, Jim killed his brother a year ago, an' the feller was jus' waitin' fer a chance to git Jim right then. I knowed that."

"Who was the big fellow who started the row, by flourishing his pistol around?" I asked.

A man on the next bed leaned forward and laughed slightly. "Well, stranger, I reckon that was me."

This sounds like the opening chapter of a piece of fiction, but we had really stumbled upon this man's cabin in the dark, and he was our host. A little spinal chill made me shiver. He had not seen us yet, and I began to wonder whether he would recognize us when the light blazed up, and whether he would know that we were ready to take part against him in the car, and what would happen, if he did. When the blaze did kindle, he was reaching for his hip, but he drew out a bottle of apple-jack and handed it over the foot of the bed.

The rest of us sat on the two beds.

Through the Bad Bend

"Somebody ought to 'a' knocked my head off," he said.

"That's so," said the younger girl, with sharp boldness. "I never seed sech doin's."

The old mountaineer, her father, gave her a quick rebuke, but the man laughed. He was sobering up, and, apparently, he had never seen us before. The young wife prepared supper, and we ate and went to bed—the ten of us in that one room. The two girls took off their shoes and stockings with frank innocence, and warmed their bare feet at the fire. The host and hostess gave up their bed to the old mountaineer and his son-in-law, and slept, like the rest of us, on the floor.

We were wakened long before day. Indeed it was pitch dark when, after a mountain custom, we stumbled to a little brook close to the cabin and washed our faces. A wood-thrush was singing somewhere in the darkness, and its cool notes had the liquid freshness of the morning. We did not wait for breakfast, so anxious were the Kentuckians to get home, or so fearful were they of abusing their host's hospitality, though the latter urged us strenuously to stay. Not a cent would he take from anybody, and I know now that he was a moonshiner, a feudsman, an outlaw, and that he was running from the sheriff at that very time.

Blue-grass and Rhododendron

With a parting pull at the apple-jack, we began, on an empty stomach, that weary climb. Not far up the mountain Breck stopped, panting, while the mountaineers were swinging on up the path without an effort, even the girls; but Breck swore that he had heart disease, and must rest. When I took part of his pack, the pretty one looked back over her shoulder and smiled at him without scorn. Both were shy, and had not spoken a dozen words with either of us. Half-way up we overtook a man and a boy, one carrying a tremendous demijohn and the other a small hand-barrel. They had been over on the Virginia side selling moonshine, and I saw the light of gladness in Breck's eye, for his own flask was wellnigh empty from returning our late host's courtesy. But both man and boy disappeared with a magical suddenness that became significant later. Already we were suspected as being revenue spies, though neither of us dreamed what the matter was.

We reached the top after daybreak, and the beauty of the sunrise over still seas of white mist and wave after wave of blue Virginia hills was unspeakable, as was the beauty of the descent on the Kentucky side, down through primeval woods of majestic oak and poplar, under a trembling world of dew-drenched leaves, and along a tumbling series of waterfalls that

Through the Bad Bend

flashed through tall ferns, blossoming laurel, and shining leaves of rhododendron.

The sun was an hour high when we reached the foot of the mountain. There the old man and the young girl stopped at a little cabin where lived the son-in-law. We, too, were pressed to stop, but we went on with the suspicious one to his house, where we got breakfast. There the people took pay, for their house was weather-boarded, and they were more civilized; or perhaps for the reason that the man thought us spies. I did not like his manner, and I got the first unmistakable hint of his suspicions after breakfast. I was down behind the barn, and he and another mountaineer came down on the other side.

"Didn't one o' them fellers come down this way?" I heard him ask.

I started to make my presence known, but he spoke too quickly, and I concluded it was best to keep still.

"No tellin' whut them damn fellers is up to. I don't like their occupation."

That is, we were the first fishermen to cast a minnow with a reel into those waters, and it was beyond the mountaineer's comprehension to understand how two men could afford to come so far and spend time and a little money just for the fun of fishing. They supposed we were fishing for profit, and later they asked us how we kept our fish fresh, and how we got them over the mountain, and where we sold them. With this idea, naturally it was a puzzle to them how we could afford to give a boy a quarter for a dozen minnows, and then, perhaps, catch not a single fish with them.

When I got back to the house, Breck was rigging his rod, with a crowd of spectators around him. Such a rod and such a fisherman had never been seen in that country before. Breck was dressed in a white tennis-shirt, blue gymnasium breeches, blue stockings, and white tennis-shoes. With a cap on his shock of black hair and a .38 revolver in his belt, he was a thing for those women to look at and to admire, and for the men to scorn—secretly, of course, for there was a look in his black eyes that forced guarded respect in any crowd. The wonder of those mountaineers when he put his rod together, fastened the reel, and tossed his hook fifty feet in the air was worth the morning's climb to see. At the same time they made fun of our rods, and laughed at the idea of getting out a big " green pyerch "—as the mountaineers call bass—with " them switches." Their method is to tie a strong line to a long hickory sapling, and, when they strike a bass, to put the stout pole over one shoulder and walk ashore with it. Before the sun

Through the Bad Bend

was over the mountain, we were wading down the stream, while two boys carried our minnows and clothes along the bank. The news of our coming went before us, and every now and then a man would roll out of the bushes with a gun and look at us with much suspicion and some wonder. For two luckless hours we cast down that too narrow and too shallow stream before we learned that there was a dam two miles farther down, and at once we took the land for it. It was after dinner when we reached it, and there the boys left us. We could not induce them to go farther. An old miller sat outside his mill across the river, looking at us with some curiosity, but no surprise, for the coming of a stranger in those mountains is always known miles ahead of him.

We told him our names and that we were from Virginia, but were natives of the Blue-grass, and we asked if he could give us dinner. His house was half a mile farther down the river, he said, but the women folks were at home, and he reckoned they would give us something to eat. When we started, I shifted my revolver from my pocket to a kodak-camera case that I had brought along to hold fishing-tackle.

"I suppose I can put this thing in here?" I said to Breck, not wanting to risk arrest for carrying concealed weapons and the confiscation of the pistol, which was valuable. Breck hesitated, and the old miller studied us keenly.

"Well," he said, "if you two air from Kanetucky, hit strikes me you ought to know the laws of yo' own State. You can carry it in thar as baggage," he added, quietly, and I knew that my question had added another fagot to the flame of suspicion kindling against us.

In half an hour we were in the cool shade of a spreading apple-tree in the miller's yard, with our bare feet in thick, cool grass, while the miller's wife and his buxom, red-cheeked daughter got us dinner. And a good dinner it was; and we laughed and cracked jokes at each other till the sombre, suspicious old lady relaxed and laughed, too, and the girl lost some of her timidity and looked upon Breck with wide-eyed admiration, while Breck ogled back outrageously.

After dinner a scowling mountaineer led a mule through the yard and gave us a surly nod. Two horsemen rode up to the gate and waited to escort us down the river. One of them carried our baggage, for no matter what he suspects, the mountaineer will do anything in the world for a stranger until the moment of actual conflict comes. In our green innocence, we thought it rather a good joke that we should be taken for revenue men, so that, Breck's flask

Through the Bad Bend

being empty, he began by telling one of the men that we had been wading the river all the morning, that the water was cold, and that, anyway, a little swallow now and then often saved a fellow from a cold and fever. He had not been able to get any from anybody—and couldn't the man *do* something? The mountaineer was touched, and he took the half-dollar that Breck gave him, and turned it over, with a whispered consultation, to one of two more horsemen that we met later on the road. Still farther on we found a beautiful hole of water, edged with a smooth bank of sand—a famous place, the men told us, for green "pyerch." Mountaineers rolled out of the bushes to watch us while we were rigging up, some with guns and some without. We left our pistols on the shore, and several examined them curiously, especially mine, which was hammerless. Later, I showed them how it worked, and explained that one advantage of it was that, in close quarters, the other man could not seize your pistol, get his finger or thumb under your hammer, and prevent you from shooting at all. This often happens in a fight, of course, and the point appealed to them strongly, but I could see that they were wondering why I should be carrying a gun that was good for close quarters, since close quarters are rarely necessary except in case of making arrests.

Blue-grass and Rhododendron

Pretty soon the two men who had gone for Breck's "moonshine" returned, and a gleam rose in Breck's eye and went quickly down. Instead of a bottle, the boy handed back the half-dollar.

"I couldn't git any," he said. He lied, of course, as we both knew, and the disappointment in Breck's face was so sincere that his companion, with a gesture that was half sympathy, half defiance, whisked a bottle from his hip.

"Well, by —— I'll give him a drink!"

It was fiery, white as water, and so fresh that we could taste the smoke in it, but it was good, and we were grateful. All the afternoon, from two to a dozen people watched us fish, but we had poor luck, which is never a surprise, fishing for bass. Perhaps the fish had gone to nesting, or the trouble may have been the light of the moon, during which they feed all night, and are not so hungry through the day; or it may have been any of the myriad reasons that make the mystery and fascination of catching bass. At another time, and from the same stream, I have seen two rods take out one hundred bass, ranging from one to five pounds in weight, in a single day. An hour by sun, we struck for the house of the old man with whom we had crossed the mountain, and, that night, we learned that we had passed through a local-

Through the Bad Bend

ity alive with moonshiners, and banded together with such system and determination that the revenue agents rarely dared to make a raid on them. We were supposed to be two spies who were expected to come in there that spring. We had passed within thirty yards of a dozen stills, and our host hinted where we might find them. We thanked him, and told him we preferred to keep as far away from them as possible. He was much puzzled. He also said that we had been in the head-quarters of a famous desperado, who was the leader of the Howard faction in the famous Howard-Turner feud. He was a non-combatant himself, but he had "feelin's," as he phrased it, for the other side. He was much surprised when we told him we were going back there next day. We had told the people we were coming back, and next morning we were foolish enough to go.

As soon as we struck the river, we saw a man with a Winchester sitting on a log across the stream, as though his sole business in life was to keep an eye on us. All that day we were never out of sight of a mountaineer and a gun; we never had been, I presume, since our first breakfast on that stream. Still, everybody was kind and hospitable and honest— how honest this incident will show. An old woman cooked dinner especially for us, and I gave her two

Blue-grass and Rhododendron

quarters. She took them, put them away, and while she sat smoking her pipe, I saw something was troubling her. She got up presently, went into a room, came back, and without a word dropped one of the quarters into my hand. Half a dollar was too much. They gave us moonshine, too, and Breck remarked casually that we were expecting to meet our friends at Uncle Job Turner's, somewhere down the river. They would have red whiskey from the Blue-grass and we would be all right. Then he asked how far down Uncle Job lived. The remark and the question occasioned very badly concealed excitement, and I wondered what had happened, but I did not ask. I was getting wary, and I had become quite sure that the fishing must be better down, very far down, that stream. When we started again, the mountaineers evidently held a quick council of war. One can hear a long distance over water at the quiet of dusk, and they were having a lively discussion about us and our business over there. Somebody was defending us, and I recognized the voice as belonging to a red-whiskered fellow, who said he had lived awhile in the Blue-grass, and had seen young fellows starting to the Kentucky River to fish for fun. "Oh, them damn fellers ain't up to nothin'," we could hear him say, with the disgust of the cosmopolitan. "I tell

Through the Bad Bend

ye, they lives in town an' they likes to git out this way!"

I have always believed that this man saved us trouble right then, for next night the mountaineers came down in a body to the house where we had last stopped. But we had gone on rather hastily, and when we reached Uncle Job Turner's, the trip behind us became more interesting than ever in retrospect. All along we asked where Uncle Job lived, and once we shouted the question across the river, where some women and boys were at work, weeding corn. As usual, the answer was another question, and always the same—what were our names? Breck yelled, in answer, that we were from Virginia, and that they would be no wiser if we should tell—an answer that will always be unwise in the mountains of Kentucky as long as moonshine is made and feuds survive. We asked again, and another yell told us that the next house was Uncle Job's. The next house was rather pretentious. It had two or three rooms, apparently, and a loft, and was weather-boarded; but it was as silent as a tomb. We shouted "Hello!" from outside the fence, which is etiquette in the mountains. Not a sound. We shouted again—once, twice, many times. It was most strange. Then we waited, and shouted again, and at last a big gray-haired old fellow slouched out and asked rather surlily what we wanted.

"Dinner."

He seemed pleased that that was all, and his manner changed immediately. His wife appeared; then, as if by magic, two or three children, one a slim, wild, dark-eyed girl of fifteen, dressed in crimson homespun. As we sat on the porch I saw her passing through the dark rooms, but always, while we were there, if I entered one door she slipped out of the other. Breck was more fortunate. He came up behind her the next day at sundown while she was dancing barefooted in the dust of the road, driving her cows home. Later I saw him in the cow-pen, helping her milk. He said she was very nice, but very shy.

We got dinner, and the old man sent after a bottle of moonshine, and in an hour he was thawed out wonderfully.

We told him where we had been, and as he slowly began to believe us, he alternately grew sobered and laughed aloud.

"Went through thar fishin', did ye? Wore yo' pistols? Axed whar thar was branches whar you could ketch minners? Oh, Lawd! Didn't ye know that the stills air al'ays up the branches? Tol' 'em *you was goin' to meet a party at my house, and stay*

Through the Bad Bend

here awhile fishin'? Oh, Lawdy! Ef that ain't a good un!"

We didn't see it, but we did later, when we knew that we had come through the "Bad Bend," which was the head-quarters of the Howard leader and his chief men; that Uncle Job was the most prominent man of the other faction, and lived farthest up the river of all the Turners; that he hadn't been up in the Bend for ten years, and that we had given his deadly enemies the impression that we were friends of his. As Uncle Job grew mellow, and warmed up in his confidences, something else curious came out. Every now and then he would look at me and say:

"I seed you lookin' at my pants." And then he would throw back his head and laugh. After he had said this for the third time, I did look at his "pants," and I saw that he was soaking wet to the thighs— why, I soon learned. A nephew of his had killed a man at the county-seat only a week before. Uncle Job had gone on his bond. When we shouted across the river, he was in the cornfield, and when we did not tell our names, he got suspicious, and, mistaking our rod-holders for guns, had supposed that his nephew had run away, and that we were officers come to arrest him. He had run down the river on the other side, had waded the stream, and was up in the loft with his

Blue-grass and Rhododendron

Winchester on us while we were shouting at his gate. He told us this very frankly. Nor would even he believe that we were fishing. He, too, thought that we were officers looking through the Bad Bend for some criminal, and the least innocent mission that struck him as plausible was that, perhaps, we might be looking over the ground to locate a railroad, or prospecting for coal veins. When Uncle Job went down the road with us the next morning, he took his wife along, so that no Howard would try to ambush him through fear of hitting a woman. And late that afternoon, when we were fishing with Uncle Job's son in some thick bushes behind the house, some women passed along in the path above us, and, seeing us, but not seeing him, scurried out of sight as though frightened. Little Job grinned.

"Them women thinks the Howards have hired you fellers to layway dad."

The next morning I lost Breck, and about noon I got a note from him, written with a trembling lead-pencil, to the effect that he believed he would fish up a certain creek that afternoon. As the creek was not more than three feet wide and a few inches deep, I knew what had happened, and I climbed one of Job's mules and went to search for him. Breck had stumbled upon a moonshine still, and, getting hilari-

Through the Bad Bend

ous, had climbed a barrel and was making to a crowd of mountaineers a fiery political speech. Breck had captured that creek, "wild-cat" still and all, and to this day I never meet a mountaineer from that region who does not ask, with a wide grin, about Breck.

When we reached the county-seat, the next day, we met the revenue deputy. He said the town was talking about two spies who were up the Fork. We told him that we must be the spies. The old miller was the brains of the Bend, he said, both in outwitting the revenue men and in planning the campaign of the Howard leader against the Turners, and he told us of several fights he had had in the Bad Bend. He said that we were lucky to come through alive; that what saved us was sticking to the river, hiring our minnows caught, leaving our pistols on the bank to be picked up by anybody, the defence of the red-whiskered man from the Blue-grass, and Breck's popularity at the still. I thought he was exaggerating—that the mountaineers, even if convinced that we were spies, would have given us a chance to get out of the country—but when he took me over to a room across the street and showed me where his predecessor, a man whom I had known quite well, was shot through a window at night and killed, I was not quite so sure.

But still another straw of suspicion was awaiting us.

Blue-grass and Rhododendron

When we reached the railroad again—by another route, you may be sure—Breck, being a lawyer, got permission for us to ride on a freight-train, and thus save a night and a day. The pass for us was technically charged to the mail service. The captain and crew of the train were overwhelmingly and mysteriously polite to us—an inexplicable contrast to the surliness with which passengers are usually treated on a freight-train. When we got off at the Gap, and several people greeted us by name, the captain laughed.

"Do you know what these boys thought you two were?" he asked, referring to his crew. "They thought you were freight 'spotters.'"

The crew laughed. I looked at Breck, and I didn't wonder. He was a ragged, unshaven tramp, and I was another.

Months later, I got a message from the Bad Bend. Breck and I mustn't come through there any more. We have never gone through there any more, though anybody on business that the mountaineers understand, *can* go more safely than he can cross Broadway at Twenty-third Street, at noon. As a matter of fact, however, there are two other forks to the Cumberland in which the fishing is very good indeed, and just now I would rather risk Broadway.

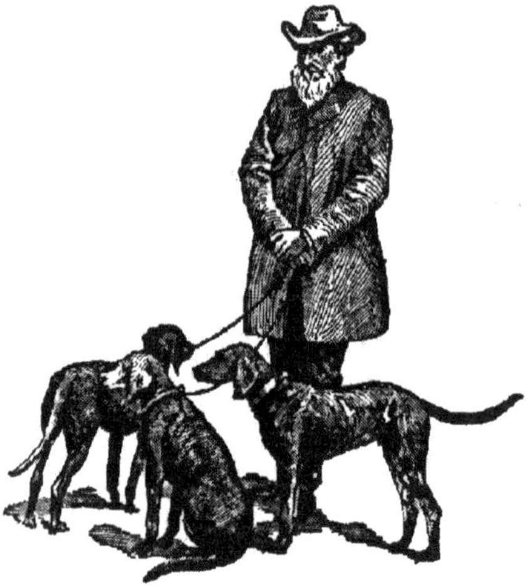

Fox-Hunting in Kentucky

I

THE Judge parted his coat-tails to the big pine-wood blaze, and, with one measuring, vertical glance, asked me two questions:

"Do you hunt coons? Do you hunt gray foxes?"

A plea of not guilty was made to both, and the Judge waved his hand.

"If you do," he said, "I decline to discuss the subject with you."

Already another fox-hunter, who was still young, and therefore not quite lost to the outer world, had warned me. "They are cranks," he said, "fox-hunters are—all of 'em."

And then he, who was yet sane, went on to tell about his hound, Red Star: how Red Star would seek a lost trail from stump to stump, or on top of a rail-fence; or, when crows cawed, would leave the trail and make for the crows; how he had once followed a fox twenty hours, and had finally gone after him into a sink-hole,

Blue-grass and Rhododendron

from which he had been rescued several days later, almost starved. On cold winter nights the young hunter would often come on the lonely figure of the old Judge, who had walked miles out of town merely to sit on the fence and listen to the hounds. Against him, the warning was particular. I made a tentative mention of the drag-hunt, in which the hounds often ran mute, and the fun was in the horse, the ride, and the fences. For a moment the Judge was reflective.

"I remember," he said, slowly, as though he were a century back in reminiscence, "that the darkies used to drag a coonskin through the woods, and run mongrels after it."

A hint of fine scorn was in his tone, but it was the scorn of the sportsman and not of the sectionalist, though the Judge, when he was only fifteen, had carried pistol and sabre after John Morgan, and was, so the General said, a moment later, the gamest man in the Confederacy.

"Why, sir, there is but one nobler animal than a long-eared, deep-mouthed, patient fox-hound—and that is a woman! Think of treating him that way! And the music is the thing! Many an old Virginian would give away a dog because his tongue was not in harmony with the rest. The chorus should be a

Fox-Hunting in Kentucky

chord. I shall never hear sweeter music, unless, by the grace of Heaven, I hear some day the choiring of angels."

I was about to speak of the Maine and Massachusetts custom of shooting the fox before the hounds, but the Judge forestalled me.

"I believe, sir, that is worse—if worse be possible. I do not know what excuse the gentlemen make. They say, I believe, that their dogs cannot catch their red fox—that no dogs can. Well, the ground up there, being rough, is favorable to the fox, but our dogs can catch him. Logan, a Kentucky dog, has just caught a Massachusetts fox for the Brunswick Fur Club, and we have much better dogs here than Logan.

"Yes," he added, tranquilly; "I believe it is generally conceded now that the Kentucky dog has taken a stand with the Kentucky horse. The winnings on the bench and in the field, the reports wherever Kentucky dogs have been sent, the advertisements in the sporting papers, all show that. Steve Walker, who, by the way, will never sell a dog, and who will buy any dog that can beat his own, has tried every strain in this country except the Wild Goose Pack of Tennessee. He has never gone outside the State without getting a worse dog. I reckon phosphate of lime has

Blue-grass and Rhododendron

something to do with it. The same natural forces in the Blue-grass region that make horses better improve the dogs. Since the war, too, we have bred with more care; we have hunted more than people elsewhere, and we have bred the dog as we have the race-horse. Why, the Walkers—ah!"—the Judge stopped to listen—"There's Steve's horn now!"

Only one man could blow that long mellow call, swelling and falling without a break, and ending like a distant echo.

"We better go, boys," he said.

Outside the hotel, the hunter's moon was tipped just over one of the many knobs from which Daniel Boone is said to have looked first over the Blue-grass land. A raindrop would have slipped from it into the red dawn just beneath. And that was the trouble, for hunters say there is never rain to drop when the moon is tipped that way. So the field trials had been given up; the country was too rough; and the elements and the local sportsmen, who hunted the ground by night that we were to hunt by day, held the effort in disfavor. That day everybody and everybody's hound were to go loose for simple fun, and the fun was beginning before dawn. In the stable-yard, darkies and mountaineers were bridling and saddling horses. The hunters were noisily coming and going from the

Fox-Hunting in Kentucky

little hotel that was a famous summer-resort in the Bath County Hills forty years ago, and, once owned by a great Kentuckian, was, the tradition goes, lost by him in a game of poker. Among them were several Bluegrass girls in derby hats, who had been in the saddle with us on the previous day from dark to dark, and on to midnight, and who were ready to do it again. There were fox-hunters from Maine, the Virginias, Ohio, and from England; and the contrasts were marked even among the Kentuckians who came from the Iroquois Club, of Lexington, with bang-tailed horses and top-boots; from the Strodes Valley Hunt Club and the Bourbon Kennels, who disdain any accoutrement on horseback that they do not wear on foot; and from the best-known fox-hunting family in the South, who dress and hunt after their own way, and whom I shall call Walkers, because they are never seen on foot. No Walker reaches the age of sixteen without being six feet high. There were four with us, and the shortest was six feet two, and weighed 185 pounds. They wore great oilskin mackintoshes, and were superbly mounted on half thoroughbreds. Not long ago they carried their native county Democratic for one friend by 250 majority. At the next election they carried it Republican by the same majority for another friend. "We own everything in common," said

Blue-grass and Rhododendron

one, who asked me to come over and spend a few months, or a year, or the rest of my natural life with him, "except our dogs." No Walker's dog will follow any other Walker, or come to his horn. All the Walkers had great, soft musical voices and gentle manners. All were church members, and, *mirabile dictu*, only one of the four touched whiskey, and he lightly. About one of them the General told a remarkable story.

This Walker, he said, got into a difficulty with another young man just after the war. The two rode into the county town, hitched their horses, and met in the court-house square. They drew their pistols, which were old-fashioned, and emptied them, each man getting one bullet. Then they drew knives. They closed in after both had been cut slightly. The other man made for Walker's abdomen, just as Walker's knife was high over his head for a terrible downward stroke. Walker had on an old army belt, and the knife struck the buckle and broke at the hilt. Walker saw it as his knife started down. He is a man of fierce passion, but even at that moment he let his knife fall and walked away.

"It's easy enough in a duel," commented the General, "when everything is cool and deliberate, to hold up if your adversary's pistol gets out of order; but in

Fox-Hunting in Kentucky

a hand-to-hand fight like that! They have been close friends ever since—naturally."

Being such a company, we rode out of the stable-yard through the frosty dawn toward the hills, which sink by and by to the gentle undulations of Blue-grass pasture and woodland.

II

IN Kentucky, the hunting of the red fox antedates the war but little. The old Kentucky fox-hound was of every color, loose in build, with open feet and a cowhide tail. He had a good nose, and he was slow, but he was fast enough for the gray fox and the deer. Somewhere about 1855 the fox-hunters discovered that their hounds were chasing something they could not catch. A little later a mule-driver came through Cumberland Gap with a young hound that he called Lead. Lead caught the eye of old General Maupin, who lived in Madison County, and whose name is now known to every fox-hunter North and South. Maupin started poor, and made a fortune in a frolic. He would go out hunting with his hounds, and would come back home with a drove of sheep and cattle. He was a keen trader, and would buy anything. He bought Lead, and, in the first chase, Lead slipped away

Blue-grass and Rhododendron

from the old deer-hounds as though he knew what he was after; and it was not long before he captured the strange little beast that had been puzzling man and dog so long. Lead was thus the first hound to catch a red fox in Kentucky; and since every fox-hound in the State worthy of the name goes back to Lead, he is a very important personage. General Maupin never learned Lead's exact origin; perhaps he did not try very hard, for he soon ran across a suspicion that Lead had been stolen. He tried other dogs from the same locality in Tennessee from which he supposed the hound came, but with no good results. Lead was a *lusus naturæ*, and old fox-hunters say that his like was never before him, and has never been since.

People came for miles to see the red fox that Lead ran down, and the event was naturally an epoch in the history of the chase in Kentucky. Nobody knows why it took the red fox so long to make up his mind to emigrate to Kentucky, not being one of the second families of Virginia, and nobody knows why he came at all. Perhaps the shrewd little beast learned that over the mountains the dogs were slow and old-fashioned, and that he could have great fun with them and die of old age; perhaps the prescience of the war moved him; but certain it is that he did not take the "Wilderness Road" until the fifties, when began the

Calling Off the Dogs.

Fox-Hunting in Kentucky

inexplicable movement of his race south and southwest. But he took the trail of the gray fox then, just as the tide-water Virginians took the trail of the pioneers, and the gray fox gave way, and went farther west, as did the pioneer, and let the little red-coated aristocrat stamp his individuality on the Bluegrass as his human brother had done. For a long while he did have fun with those clumsy old hounds, running a hundred easy lengths ahead, dawdling time and again past his den, disdaining to take refuge, and turning back to run past the hounds when they had given up the chase—great fun, until old Lead came. After that, General Maupin and the Walkers imported Martha and Rifler from England, and, since then, the red fox has been kept to his best pace so steadily that he now shows a proper respect for even a young Kentucky fox-hound. He was a great solace after the war, for Kentucky was less impoverished than other Southern States, horses were plentiful, it was inexpensive to keep hounds, and other game was killed off. But fox-hunting got into disrepute. Hunting in Southern fashion requires a genius for leisure that was taken advantage of by ne'er-do-weels and scapegraces, young and old, who used it as a cloak for idleness, drinking, and general mischief. They broke down the farmer's fences, left his gates open, trampled his grain, and

Blue-grass and Rhododendron

brought a reproach on the fox-hunter that is alive yet. It is dying rapidly, however, and families like the Clays, of Bourbon, the Robinsons and Hamiltons, of Mount Sterling, the Millers and Winns, of Clark, and the Walkers, of Garrard, are lifting the chase into high favor. Hitherto, the hunting has been done individually. Now hunt clubs are being formed. Chief among them are the Bourbon Kennels, the Strodes Valley Hunt Club, and the Iroquois Club, the last having been in existence for ten years. This club does not confine itself to foxes, but is democratic enough to include coons and rabbits.

Except in Maine and Massachusetts, where the fox is shot before the hounds, fox-hunting in the North is modelled after English ways. In Kentucky and elsewhere in the South, it is almost another sport. The Englishman wants his pack uniform in color, size, tongue, and speed—a hound that is too fast must be counted out. The Kentuckian wants his hound to leave the rest behind, if he can. He has no whipper-in, no master of the hounds. Each man cries on his own dog. Nor has he any hunting terms, like "cross-country riding," or "riding to hounds." To hunt for the pleasure of the ride is his last thought. The fun is in the actual chase, in knowing the ways of the plucky little animal, in knowing the hounds individually, and the tongue of each, in the competition of one man's dog with another, or of favorites in the same pack. It is not often that the hounds are followed steadily. The stake-and-ridered fences everywhere, and the barbed wire in the Blue-grass, would make following impossible, even if it were desirable. Instead, the hunters ride from ridge to ridge to wait, to listen, and to see. The Walkers hunt chiefly at night. The fox is then making his circuit for food, and the scent is better. Less stock is moving about to be frightened, or among which the fox can confuse the hounds. The music has a mysterious sweetness, the hounds hunt better, it seems less a waste of time, and it is more picturesque. At night the hounds trot at the horses' heels until a fire is built on some ridge. Then they go out to hunt a trail, while the hunters tie their horses in the brush, and sit around the fire telling stories until some steady old hound gives tongue.

"There's old Rock! Whoop-ee! Go it, old boy!" Only he doesn't say "old boy" exactly. The actual epithet is bad, though it is endearing. It reaches old Rock if he is three miles away, and the crowd listens.

"There's Ranger! Go it, Alice, old girl! Lead's ahead!"

Blue-grass and Rhododendron

Then they listen to the music. Sometimes the fox takes an unsuspected turn, and they mount and ride for another ridge; and the reckless, daredevil race they make through the woods in the dark is to an outsider pure insanity. Sometimes a man will want to go on one side of the tree when his horse prefers another, and the man is carried home senseless. Sometimes a horse is killed, but no lesson is learned. The idea prevails that the more reckless one is, the better is his chance to get through alive, and it seems to hold good. In their county, the Walkers have both hills and blue-grass in which to hunt. The fox, they say, is leaving the hills, and taking up his home in the plantations, because he can get his living there with more ease. They hunt at least three nights out of the week all the year around, and they say that May is the best month of the year. The fox is rearing her young then. The hunters build a fire near a den, the she-fox barks to attract the attention of the dogs, and the race begins. At that time, the fox will not take a straight line to the mountains and end the chase as at other times of the year, but will circle about the den. It is true, perhaps, that at such times the male fox relieves the mother and takes his turn in keeping the hounds busy. The hunters thus get their pleasure without being obliged to leave their camp-fire.

Listening to the Music of the Dogs.

Fox-Hunting in Kentucky

Rarely at this time is the fox caught, and provided he has had the fun of the chase, the Kentucky hunter is secretly glad, I believe, that the little fellow has gone scot-free.

Such being the hunt, there is, of course, no ceremony whatever in its details; it is "go as you please," as to horse, way of riding, dress, and riding accoutrements. The effect is picturesque and individual. Each man dresses, usually, as he dresses on foot, his seat is the military seat, his bridle has one rein, his horse is bridle-wise, and his hunter is his saddle-horse. The Kentuckian does not like to trot anywhere in the saddle. He prefers to go in a "rack," or a running walk. His horse, when he jumps at all, does not take fences in his stride, but standing. And I have yet to see anything more graceful than the slow rear, the calculating poise, the leap wholly from the hind feet, and the quick, high gather to clear the fence. It is not impossible to find a horse that will feel for the top rail with his knees, and if they are not high enough, he will lift them higher before making his leap. I have known of one horse that, while hitched to a stake-and-ridered fence, would jump the fence without unhitching himself.

It was an odd and interesting crowd that went through the woods that morning—those long-maned,

Blue-grass and Rhododendron

long-tailed horses, and their riders, the giants in slouched hats and oilskins, the pretty girls with a soft fire of anticipation in their straight, clear eyes—especially to the hunters from the East, and to the Englishman with his little hunting-saddle, his short stirrups, his top-boots thrust into them to the heels, and his jockey-like seat—just as he was odd to them. I saw one Kentuckian double on his horse, laughing at the apparent inefficiency of his appearance, little knowing that in the English hunting-field the laugh would have been the other way.

To the stranger, the hounds doubtless looked small and wiry, being bred for speed, as did the horses, because of the thoroughbred blood in them, livery hacks though most of them were. Perhaps he was most surprised at the way those girls dashed through the woods, and the way the horses galloped over stones and roots, and climbed banks, for which purpose the Eastern hunter would have been inadequate, through lack of training. The Southern way of riding doubtless struck him as slovenly—the loose rein, the toes in the stirrups (which upheld merely the weight of the legs), the easy, careless, graceful seat; but he soon saw that it was admirably adapted to the purpose at hand—staying on the horse and getting out all that there was in him. For when the Southern fox-hunter starts

Fox-Hunting in Kentucky

after his hounds through wood and thicket, in daylight or dark, you know whence came the dashing horsemanship that gave the South a marked advantage some thirty years ago. And when he gets warmed up, and opens his throat to cry on his favorite hound, you know at last the origin of the "rebel yell," and you hear it again but little changed to-day.

III

WITHIN ten minutes after the dogs were unleashed, there was an inspiriting little brush through the woods. A mule went down, and his rider executed a somersault. Another rider was unhorsed against a tree. How the girls came through with their skirts was a mystery; but there they were, eager and smiling, when we halted on the edge of a cleared field. The hounds were circling far to the left. The General pointed to a smouldering fire which the local sportsmen had used through the night.

"It's an old trail," he said, and we waited there, as we waited anywhere, with an unwearying patience that would have thrown an Eastern hunter into hysteria.

"No, sir," said the General, courteously, in answer to a question; "I never sell a fox-dog; I consider him a member of my household. It would be a sacrilege to sell him." Then he continued learnedly and calmly:

"As is the fox, so in time is the dog; that is the theory. The old English dog was big-boned, coarse, and heavy, and he had to have greyhound blood before he could catch the English red fox. The English dog has always been, and is now, inadequate for the American red fox. By selection, by breeding winner with winner, we have got a satisfactory dog, and the more satisfactory he is, the more is he like the fox, having become smaller in size, finer in bone, and more compact in shape. The hunted moulds the hunter: the American red fox is undoubtedly superior to the English red fox in speed, endurance, and stratagem, and he has made the American dog superior. The principle was illustrated when old Lead came over to Cumberland; for he was rather small and compact, his hair was long and his brush heavy, though his coat was coal-black except for a little tan about the face and eyes. The Virginia red fox had already fashioned Lead."

The hounds were coming back now; they were near when the music ceased. The great yellow figure of a Walker was loping toward them through the frost-tipped sedge, with his hat in his hand and his thick gray hair catching the first sunlight. The General was right; the trail was old, and it was lost. As we rode across the field, however, an old hound gave tongue. Sharp, quick music began, and ceased just as another Walker was reaching down into his trousers' pocket for his plug of tobacco.

"I believe that was a rabbit," he said. "I'm going over there and knock old Rock in the head." Without taking his hand from his pocket, he touched his horse, and the animal rose in his tracks, poised, and leaped, landing on a slippery bank. The plug of tobacco was in one corner of the rider's mouth when both struck the road. He had moved in his saddle no more than if his horse had stepped over a log. Nothing theatrical was intended. The utter nonchalance of the performance was paralyzing. He did not reach old Rock. Over to the right, another hound raised so significant a cry that Rock, with an answering bay, went for him. In a moment they were sweeping around a knoll to the right, and the third Walker turned his horse through the sedge, loping easily, his hat still in his hand, a mighty picture on horseback; and as I started after him, I saw the fourth brother scramble up a perpendicular bank twice the length of his horse—each man gone according to his own judgment. I followed the swinging black hat, and caught up, and we halted in the woods to listen, both jerking the reins to keep the horses from champing their bits. One peculiar, deep, musical tongue rose above the pack's cry. The big Walker stood in his stirrup, with his face uplifted, and I saw in it what fox-hunting means to the Kentuckian. Had he been looking into heaven, his face could not have been more rapt.

"That's Rock!" he said, breathlessly, and then he started through the woods. He weighed over 200, and was six feet four. A hole through the woods that was big enough for him, was, I thought, big enough for me, and I had made up my mind to follow him half an hour, anyhow. My memory of that ride is a trifle confused. I saw the big yellow oilskin and the thick gray hair ahead of me, whisking around trees and stumps, and over rocks and roots. I heard a great crashing of branches and a clatter of stones. Every jump something rapped me across the breast or over the head; my knees grazed trees on each side; a thorn dug into my face not far from one eye; and then I lay down on my horse's neck and thought of my sins. I did not know what it was all about, but I learned when I dared to lift my head. We had been running for a little hollow between the hills to see the fox pass, but we were too quick. Several

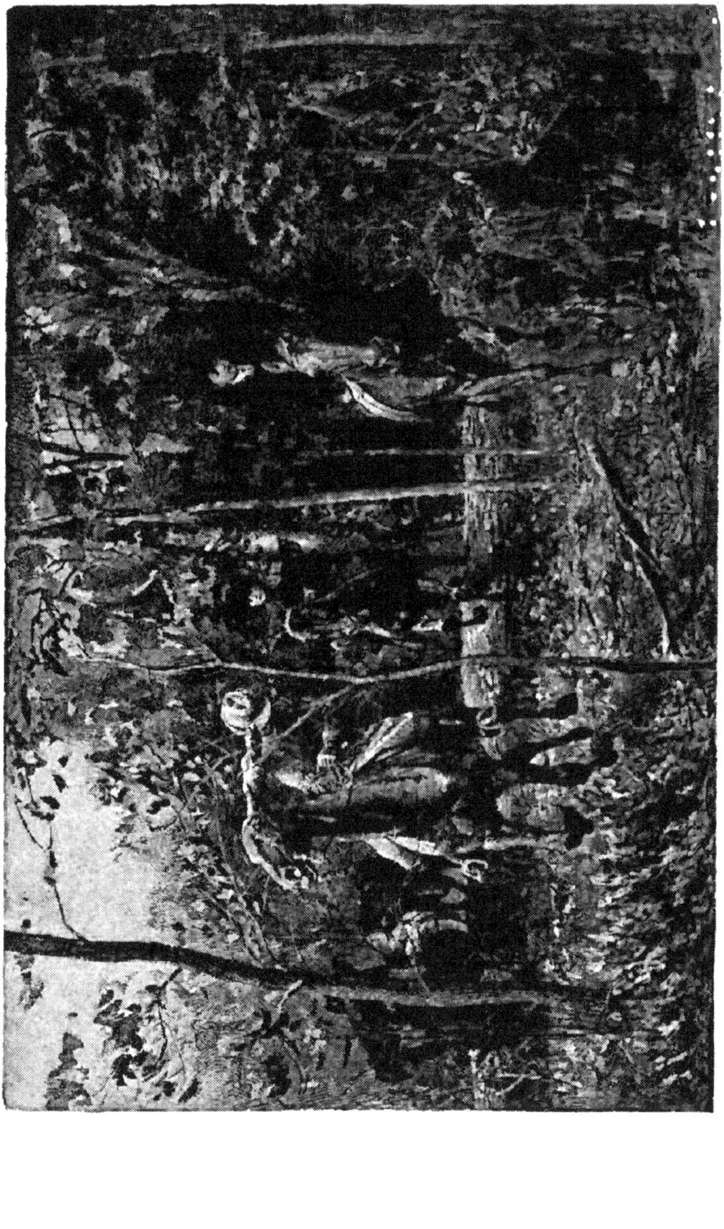

Fox-Hunting in Kentucky

hunters had crossed the trail before the hounds, and fox and scent were lost.

"You've bu'sted up the chase," said a hunter, with deep disgust.

"Who—we?" said the Walker. "Why, we have just been riding quietly up the ridge, haven't we?" *Quietly*—that was his idea of riding quietly!

I told the General about that ride, and the General laughed. "That's *him*," he said, with ungrammatical emphasis. "He's fifty-three now, but he's the hardest hunter in this State to follow."

We had to end the chase that day, and we went back to the hotel, early in the afternoon, so disheartened that the General threw his pride and his hunting traditions to the wind, and swore with a beautiful oath that the ladies should have a chase. He got a mountaineer to climb a mule and drag a coonskin around the little valley. The natives brought in their dogs, and entered them for a quart of whiskey. The music started, and Logan was allowed to let out his noble length for exercise, and Patsy Powell slipped her leash and got away, while her master swore persistently that she was running because the others were—that she scorned the scent of a drag, and would hardly run a gray fox, let alone the skin of a coon. Logan came in ahead; but a native got the whiskey, and in half an hour every one of his friends owned the best dog in the county.

That last night, after a game of blind-man's-buff, we had intersectional toasts and congratulations, and welcomes to come again. The conditions had all been antagonistic. It was too early; it was too dry; and there were many other reasons.

The man from the Brunswick Fur Club explained that in his country the sportsmen shot the foxes because the hounds could not catch them fast enough. The foxes were so thick up there that the people could hardly raise a Thanksgiving turkey. So they shot them to appease the farmers, whom they had to fight annually in the Legislature to prevent them from having the fox exterminated by law as a pest. The Southern sportsmen were glad to hear that, and drank to his health, and argued that the solution of the difficulty was to try more dogs like Logan. Then everybody discussed phases and problems of the chase that emphasized the peculiarities of hunting in the South —how the hounds, like the race-horse, have grown lighter, more rangy in form, smaller, solider in bone; and how, in spite of the increase in speed, they yet win by bottom, rather than by speed; that it was, after all, a question of the condition of the fox, whether he was gorged or not; that rough ground

Fox-Hunting in Kentucky

being favorable to the fox, more kills were made south of Virginia, because the ground is favorable to the hound; how, since the war, the breeding has been toward better feet, rougher hair, better brush, gameness, nose, and speed. Yet the Walkers say that hounds are not as good as they were twenty years ago; that the English dogs are tougher and have more bottom and less nose and speed; that the half thorough-bred makes the best hunter, the thorough-bred being too high-strung, too fretful; that the right proportion of English blood in the hound is one-fourth. And everybody wondered why some Kentucky horseman has never bred hunters for the Eastern market, arguing that the Kentucky hunter should excel, as the race-horse and the trotter have excelled.

One and another told how a fox will avoid a corn-field, because a muddy tail impedes him; how he will swim a creek simply to wash it out; and how, in Florida, he will swim a river to escape the dogs, knowing that they will not follow him through fear of the alligators. How he will turn up-stream when he is not hard pressed, and down-stream when he is. Does the red fox actually kill out the gray? One man had come on the fresh-bitten carcass of a gray in the snow, and, about it, there was not another sign than the track of a red fox. Or, does the gray disappear because he is more easily caught, or does an instinctive terror of the red drive the gray off to other hunting-grounds? A hunter declared that a full-grown gray would show mortal terror of a red cub. Is the red fox a coward, or is he the only sporting member of the animal kingdom? Does he really enjoy the chase? Many had seen him climb a stump, or fence, to look back and listen to the music. One man claimed that he often doubled out of curiosity to see where the dogs were, though another had seen a fox go through the window of a deserted house, through the floor, and out under it; and in doubling, go through it just the other way. He always did that, and that did not look like curiosity. Several had known a fox, after the hounds had given up the chase and turned homeward, to turn, too, and run past the dogs with a plain challenge to try it again. Another said he had known a fox to run till tired, and then let a fresh fox take up the trail, and lead the hounds on while he rested in a thicket twenty yards away. All except one hunter had known foxes to run past their holes several times during the chase, and often to be caught within one or two hundred yards of a den. One opinion was that a fox would not go into his hole because he was too hot and would smother; another said he was game. But the doubting hunter, an old gentleman who was nearly

Fox-Hunting in Kentucky

seventy, and who had kept close behind the hounds on a big sorrel, with an arm that had been thrown out of place at the shoulder only the night before, declared that most fox-stories were moonshine, that the fox was a sneaking little coward, and would make for a hole as soon as he heard a dog bark. There was one man who knew another man who had seen a strange thing. All the others had heard of it, and many believed it. A fox, hard pressed, had turned, and, with every bristle thrown forward, had run back, squealing piteously, into the jaws of the pack.

"That's a bluff game," said the old hunter.

"No," said another; "he knew that his end had come, and he went to meet it with his colors flying, like the dead-game little sport that he is."

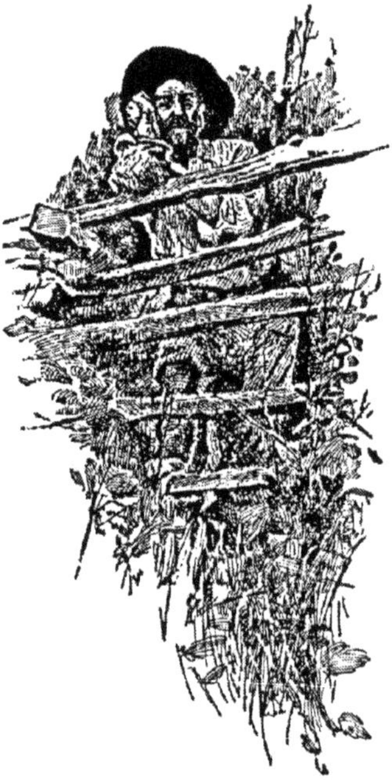

To the Breaks of Sandy

DOWN in the southwestern corner of Virginia, and just over the Kentucky line, are the Gap and "The Gap"—the one made by nature and the other by man. One is a ragged gash down through the Cumberland Mountains, from peak to water level; and the other is a new little, queer little town, on a pretty plateau which is girdled by two running streams that loop and come together like the framework of an ancient lute. Northeast the range runs, unbroken by nature and undisturbed by man, until it crumbles at the Breaks of Sandy, seventy miles away. There the bass leaps from rushing waters, and there, as nowhere else this side of the Rockies, is the face of nature wild and shy.

It was midsummer, the hour was noon, and we were bound for the Breaks of Sandy, seventy miles away.

No similar aggregate of man, trap, and beast had ever before penetrated those mountain wilds. The wagon was high-seated and the team was spiked, with Rock and Ridgling as wheel horses, Diavolo as

Blue-grass and Rhododendron

leader, and Dolly, a half-thorough-bred, galloping behind under Sam, the black cook, and a wild Western saddle, with high pommels, heavily hooded stirrups, hand-worked leather, and multitudinous straps and shaking rawhide strings; and running alongside, Tiger, bull-terrier. Any man who was at Andover, Cornell, or Harvard during certain years will, if he sees these lines, remember Tiger.

As for the men—there was Josh, ex-captain of a Kentucky Horse Guard, ex-captain of the volunteer police force back at "The Gap," and, like Henry Clay, always captain whenever and wherever there was anything to be done and more than one man was needed to do it; now, one of the later-day pioneers who went back over the Cumberland, not many years ago, to reclaim a certain wild little corner of old Virginia, and then, as now, the first man and the leading lawyer of the same. There was another Kentuckian, fresh from the Blue-grass—Little Willie, as he was styled on this trip—being six feet three in his bare feet, carrying 190 pounds of bone and muscle; champion heavy-weight with his fists in college (he could never get anybody to fight with him), centre-rush in foot-ball, with this grewsome record of broken bones: collar-bone, one leg, one knee three times, and three teeth smashed—smashed by

To the Breaks of Sandy

biting through his nose guard against each other when he set his jaws to break through a hostile line. Also, Willie was ex-bugler of a military school, singer of coon songs unrivalled, and with other accomplishments for which there is no space here to record. There was Dan, boy-manager of a mighty coal company, good fellow, and of importance to the dog-lover as the master of Tiger. I include Tiger here, because he was so little less than human. There are no words to describe Tiger. He was prepared for Yale at Andover, went to Cornell in a pet, took a post-graduate course at Harvard, and, getting indifference and world-weariness there, followed his master to pioneer in the Cumberland. Tiger has a white collar, white-tipped tail, white feet; his body is short, strong, close-knit, tawny, ringed; and his peculiar distinctions are intelligence, character, magnetism. All through the mountains Tiger has run his fifty miles a day behind Dolly, the thorough-bred; so that, in a radius of a hundred miles, there is nobody who does not know that dog. Still, he never walks unless it is necessary, and his particular oscillation is between the mines and "The Gap," ten miles apart. Being a coal magnate, he has an annual pass and he always takes the train—alone, if he pleases—changing cars three times and paying no attention, until his stations are called.

Blue-grass and Rhododendron

Sometimes he is too weary to go to a station, so he sits down on the track and waits for the train. I have known the engineer of a heavily laden freight-train to slacken up when he saw Tiger trotting ahead between the rails, and stop to take him aboard, did Tiger but nod on him. I have never seen man, woman, or child, of respectable antecedents, whom that dog didn't love, and nobody, regardless of antecedents, who didn't love that dog.

Such, we rattled out of "The Gap" that midsummer noon. Northward, through the Gap, a cloud of dun smoke hung over the Hades of coke ovens that Dan had planted in the hills. On the right was the Ridge, heavy with beds of ore. Straight ahead was a furnace, from which the coke rose as pale-blue smoke and the ore gave out a stream of molten iron. Farther on, mountains to the right and mountains to the left came together at a little gap, and toward that point we rattled up Powell's Valley—smiling back at the sun; furnace, ore-mine, coke-cloud, and other ugly signs of civilization dropping behind us fast, and our eyes set toward one green lovely spot that was a shrine of things primeval.

In the wagon we had a tent, and things to eat, and a wooden box that looked like a typewriter case, under lock and key, and eloquently inscribed:

To the Breaks of Sandy

"Glass, 2 gal." It is a great way to carry the indispensable—in a wagon—and I recommend it to fishermen.

At the foot of the first mountain was a spring and we stopped to water the horses and unlock that case. Twenty yards above, and to one side of the road, a mountaineer was hanging over the fence, looking down at us.

"Have a drink?" said Josh.

"Yes," he drawled, "if ye'll fetch it up."

"Come an' get it," said Josh, shortly.

"Are you sick?" I asked.

"Sort o' puny."

We drank.

"Have a drink?" said Josh once more.

"If ye'll fetch it up."

Josh drove the cork home with the muscular base of his thumb.

"I'm damned if I do."

Dan whistled to Diavolo, and we speculated. It was queer conduct in the mountaineer—why didn't he come down?

"I don't know," said Dan.

"He really came down for a drink," I said, knowing the mountaineer's independence, "and he wanted to prove to himself and to us that he didn't."

Blue-grass and Rhododendron

"A smart Alec," said Little Willie.

"A plain damn fool," said Josh.

Half an hour later we were on top of the mountain, in the little gap where the mountains came together. Below us the valley started on its long, rich sweep southward, and beyond were the grim shoulders of Black Mountains, which we were to brush now and then on our way to the "Breaks."

There Dan put Tiger out of the wagon and made him walk. After three plaintive whines to his master to show cause for such an outrage, Tiger dropped nose and eyes to the ground and jogged along with such human sullenness that Willie was led to speak to him. Tiger paid no attention. I called him and Dan called him. Tiger never so much as lifted eye or ear, and Willie watched him, wondering.

"Why, that dog's got a grouch," he said at last, delightedly. "I tell you he's got a grouch." It was Willie's first observation of Tiger. Of course he had a "grouch" as distinctly as a child who is old enough to show petulance with dignity. And having made us feel sufficiently mean, Tiger dropped quite behind, as though to say: "I'm gettin' kind o' tired o' this. Now 'It's come here, Tiger,' and 'Stick in the mud, Tiger,' and straightway again, 'Tiger, come here.' I don't like it. I'd go home if it weren't for Dolly and

To the Breaks of Sandy

this nigger here, whom I reckon I've got to watch. But I'll stick in the mud." And he did.

At dusk we passed through Norton, where Talt Hall, desperado, killed his thirteenth and last man, and on along a rocky, muddy, Stygian-black road to Wise Court-house, where our police guard from "The Gap," with Josh as captain, guarded Talt for one month to keep his Kentucky clan from rescuing him. And there we told Dan and the big Kentuckian how banker, broker, lawyer, and doctor left his business and his home, cut port-holes in the courthouse, put the town under martial law, and, with twenty men with Winchesters in the rude box that enclosed the scaffold, and a cordon of a hundred more in a circle outside, to keep back a thousand mountaineers, thus made possible the first hanging that the county had ever known. And how, later, in the same way we hung old Doc Taylor, Hall's enemy—Swedenborgian preacher, herb doctor, revenue officer, and desperado—the "Red Fox of the Mountains."

The two listeners were much interested, for, in truth, that police guard of gentlemen who hewed strictly to the line of the law, who patrolled the streets of "The Gap" with billy, whistle, and pistol, knocking down toughs, lugging them to the calaboose, appearing in court against them next morning, and maintaining a fund for the prosecution of them in the higher courts, was as unique and successful an experiment in civilization as any borderland has ever known.

Next day we ran the crests of long ridges and struck good roads, and it was then that we spiked Rock and Ridgling, with Diavolo as leader.

"Tool 'em!" shouted Willie, and we "tooled" joyously. A coach-horn was all that we lacked, and we did not lack that long. Willie evolved one from his unaided throat, in some mysterious way that he could not explain, but he did the tooting about as well as it is ever done with a horn. It was hot, and the natives stared. They took us for the advance-guard of a circus.

"Where are you goin' to show?" they shouted. We crossed ridges, too, tooling recklessly about the edges of precipices and along roads scarcely wide enough for one wagon—Dan swinging to the brake with one hand and holding Josh in the driver's seat with the other—Willie and I speculating, meanwhile, how much higher the hind wheel could go from the ground before the wagon would overturn. It was great fun, and dangerous.

"Hank Monks is not in it," said Willie.

The brake required both of Dan's hands just then and Josh flew out into space and landed on

They took us for the advance-guard of a circus.

To the Breaks of Sandy

his shoulder, some ten feet down the mountain, unhurt.

Rock, though it was his first work under harness, was steady as a plough-horse. Ridgling now and then would snort and plunge and paw, getting one foot over the wagon tongue. Diavolo, like his master, was a born leader, or we should have had trouble indeed.

That night we struck another county-seat, where the court-house had been a brick bone of contention for many, many years—two localities claiming the elsewhere undisputed honor, for the reason that they alone had the only two level acres in the county on which a court-house could stand. A bitter fight it was, and they do say that not many years ago, in a similar conflict, the opposing factions met to decide the question with fist and skull—150 picked men on each side—a direct and curious survival of the ancient wager of battle. The women prevented the fight. Over in Kentucky there would have been a bloody feud. At that town we had but fitful sleep. Certain little demons of the dark, which shall be nameless, marked us, as they always mark fresh victims, for their own.

"I'll bet they look over the register every night," said Willie—baring a red-splotched brawny arm next morning.

Blue-grass and Rhododendron

"Wingless victory!" he said, further.

And then on. Wilder and ever wilder, next day, grew the hills and woods and the slitting chasms between them. First one hind wheel dished—we braced it with hickory saplings. Then the other—we braced that. The harness broke—Dan mended that. A horse cast a shoe—Josh shod him then and there. These two were always tinkering, and were happy. Inefficiency made Willie and me miserable—it was plain that we were to be hewers of wood and drawers of water on that trip, and we were.

And still wilder and ever wilder was the face of Nature, which turned primeval—turned Greek. Willie swore he could see the fleeting shapes of nymphs in the dancing sunlight and shadows under the beeches. Where the cane-rushes shivered and shook along the bank of a creek, it was a satyr chasing a dryad through them; and once—it may have been the tinkle of water—but I was sure I heard her laugh float from a dark little ravine high above, where she had fled to hide. No wonder! We were approaching the most isolated spot, perhaps, this side of the Rockies. If this be hard to believe, listen. Once we stopped at a cabin, and Sam, the black cook, went in for a drink of water. A little girl saw him and was thrown almost into convulsions of terror. She had

To the Breaks of Sandy

never seen a negro before. Her mother had told her, doubtless, that the bad man would get her some day and she thought Sam was the devil and that he had come for her. And this in Virginia. I knew there were many white people in Virginia, and all throughout the Cumberland, who had never seen a black man, and why they hate him as they do has always been a mystery, especially as they often grant him social equality, even to the point of eating at the same table with him, though the mountaineer who establishes certain relations with the race that is still tolerated in the South, brings himself into lasting disgrace. Perhaps the hostility reaches back to the time when the poor white saw him a fatal enemy, as a slave, to the white man who must work with his hands. And yet, to say that this competition with the black man, along with a hatred of his aristocratic master, was the reason for the universal Union sentiment of the Southern mountaineer during the war is absurd. Competition ceased nearly a century ago. Negro and aristocrat were forgotten—were long unknown. No historian seems to have guessed that the mountaineer was loyal because of 1776. The fight for the old flag in 1812 and the Mexican War helped, but 1776 was enough to keep him loyal to this day; for to-day, in life, character, customs, speech, and conviction, he is practically what he was then. But a change is coming now, and down in a little hollow we saw, suddenly, a startling sign—a frame house with an upper balcony, and, moving along that balcony, a tall figure in a pink ungirded Mother Hubbard. And, mother of all that is modern, we saw against the doorway below her—a bicycle. We took dinner there and the girl gave me her card. It read:

AMANDA TOLLIVER,

EXECUTRIX TO JOSIAH TOLLIVER.

Only that was not her name. She owned coal lands, was a woman of judgment and business, and realizing that she could not develop them alone, had advertised for a partner in coal, and, I was told, in love as well. Anyhow there were numerous pictures of young men around, and I have a faint suspicion that as we swung over the brow of the hill, we might have been taken for suitors four. She had been to school at the county-seat where we spent the first night, and had thus swung into the stream of Progress. She had live gold fish in a glass tank and jugs with plants growing out of the mouth and out of holes in the sides. And she had a carpet in the parlor and fire-screens of red calico and red plush albums, a birthday book, and, of

Along roads scarce wide enough for one wagon.

course, a cottage organ. It was all prophetic, I suppose, and the inevitable American way toward higher things; and it was at once sad and hopeful.

Just over the hill, humanity disappeared again and Nature turned primeval—turned Greek again. And again nymphs and river gods began their play. Pretty soon a dryad took human shape in some blackberry bushes, and Little Willie proceeded to take mythological shape as a faun. We moderns jollied him on the metamorphosis.

The Breaks were just ahead. Somewhere through the green thickness of poplar, oak, and maple, the river lashed and boiled between gray bowlders, eddied and danced and laughed through deep pools, or leaped in waves over long riffles, and we turned toward the low, far sound of its waters. A slip of a bare-footed girl stepped from the bushes and ran down the wood-path, and Willie checked her to engage in unnecessary small talk and to ask questions whereof he knew the answers as well as she—all leading to the final one.

"What's your name?" Unlike her hill-sisters, the girl was not shy.

"Melissa."

Shades of Hymettus, but it was fitting. There were blackberry stains about her red lips. Her eyes had the gloom of deep woods and shone from the darkness of her tumbled hair—tumbled it was, like an oat-field I had seen that morning after a wind and rain storm that swept it all night long.

"Melissa!" Willie said softly, once, twice, three times; and his throat gurgled with poetic delight in the maid and the name. I think he would have said "Prithee" and addressed her some more, but just then a homespun mother veered about the corner of a log cabin, and Melissa fled. Willie thought he had scared her.

"On the way to the Breaks," he said—"my first." We hurried the stricken youth on and pitched camp below the cabin, and on a minnow branch that slipped past low willows and under rhododendrons and dropped in happy water-falls into the Breaks, where began a vertical turreted ledge, hundreds of feet high, that ran majestically on—miles on.

There Willie at once developed unwonted vim. We needed milk and butter and eggs, so he left me to hew wood and draw water while he strode back to the cabin, and Melissa after them; and he made contracts for the same daily—he would go for them himself—and hired all Melissa's little brothers and sisters to pick blackberries for us.

Then came the first supper in the woods and draughts from the typewriter case, the label of which

To the Breaks of Sandy

Willie proceeded to alter, because the level of the fluid was sinking, and as a tribute to Melissa.

"Glass—1 gal."

It takes little to make humor in the woods. Followed sweet pipes under the stars, thickening multitudinously straight overhead, where alone we could see them.

Something was troubling Josh that night and I could see that he hesitated about delivering himself—but he did.

"Have you fellows—er—ever noticed—er—that when men get out in the woods they—er—at once begin to swear?" Each one of us had noticed that fact. Josh looked severely at me and severely at Dan and at Willie—not observing that we were looking severely at him.

"Well," he said, with characteristic decision, "I think you ought to stop it."

There was a triangular howl of derision.

"We?" I said.

"We!" said Dan.

"*We!*" yelled Willie.

Josh laughed — he had not heard the rattling fire of picturesque expletives that he had been turning loose on Rock and Ridgling since we left the Gap.

However, we each agreed to be watchful—of the others.

By the by, Willie knocked the ashes from his pipe and picked up a pail—the mother's pail in which he had brought the milk down to camp.

"I reckon they'll need this," he said, thoughtfully. "Don't you think they'll need this?" I was sure they would, and as Willie's colossal shoulders disappeared through the bushes we chuckled, and at the fire Sam, the black cook, snickered respectfully. Willie did not know the lark habits of the mountaineer. We could have told him that Melissa was in bed, but we wickedly didn't. He was soon back, and looking glum. We chuckled some more.

That night a snake ran across my breast—I suppose it was a snake—a toad beat a tattoo on Willie's broad chest, a horse got tangled in the guy-ropes, Josh and Dan swore sleepily, and long before the sun flashed down into our eyes, a mountaineer, Melissa's black-headed sire, brought us minnows which he had insisted on catching without help. Willie wondered at his anxious spirit of lonely accommodation, but it was no secret to the rest of us. The chances were that he was a moonshiner, and that he had a "still" within a mile of our camp—perhaps within a hundred yards; for moonshine stills are always located on little

To the Breaks of Sandy

running streams like the one into which we dipped our heads that morning.

After breakfast, we went down that shaded little stream into the Breaks, where, æons ago, the majestic Cumberland met its volcanic conqueror, and, after a heaving conflict, was tumbled head and shoulders to the lower earth, to let the pent-up waters rush through its shattered ribs, and where the Big Sandy grinds through them to-day, with a roar of freedom that once must have shaken the stars. It was ideal—sun, wind, rock, and stream. The water was a bit milky; there were eddies and pools, in sunlight and in shadow, and our bait, for a wonder, was perfect—chubs, active cold-water chubs and military minnows—sucker-shaped little fellows, with one brilliant crimson streak from gill to base of tail. And we did steady, faithful work—all of us—including Tiger, who, as Willie said, was a "fisher-dog to beat the band." But is there any older and sadder tale for the sportsman than to learn, when he has reached one happy hunting-ground, that the game is on another, miles away? Thus the Indian's idea of heaven sprang! For years and years Josh and I had been planning to get to the Breaks. For years we had fished the three forks of the Cumberland, over in Kentucky, with brilliant success, and the man who had been to the Breaks always smiled

Blue-grass and Rhododendron

indulgently when we told our tales, and told, in answer, the marvellous things possible in the wonderful Breaks. Now we were at the Breaks, and no sooner there than we were ready, in great disgust, to get away. We investigated. There had been a drought, two years before, and the mountaineers had sledged the bass under the rocks and had slaughtered them. There had been saw-mills up the river and up its tributaries, and there had been dynamiting. We found catfish a-plenty, but we were not after catfish. We wanted that king of mountain waters, the black bass, and we wanted him to run from one pound to five pounds in weight and to fight, like the devil that he is, in the clear cold waters of the Cumberland. Nobody showed disappointment more bitter than Tiger. To say that Tiger was eager and expectant is to underrate that game little sport's intelligence and his power to catch moods from his master. At first he sat on the rocks, with every shining tooth in his head a finished cameo of expectant delight, and he watched the lines shaking in the eddies as he would watch a hole for a rat, or another dog for a fight. When the line started cutting through the water and the musical hum of the reel rose, Tiger knew as well as his master just what was happening.

"Let him run, Dan," he would gurgle, delightedly.

At the Breaks.

To the Breaks of Sandy

We all knew plainly that that was what he said. "Give him plenty of line. Don't strike yet—not yet. Don't you know that he's just running for a rock? Now he's swallowing the minnow—head first. Off he goes again—now's your time, man, now—wow!"

When the strike came and the line got taut and the rod bent, Tiger would begin to leap and bark at the water's edge. As Dan reeled in and the fish would flash into the air, Tiger would get frantic. When his master played a bass and the fish cut darting circles forward and back, with the tip of the rod as a centre for geometrical evolutions, Tiger would have sprung into the water, if he had not known better. And when the bass was on the rocks, Tiger sprang for him and brought him to his master, avoiding the hook as a wary lad will look out for the sharp horns of a mudcat. But the bass were all little fellows, and Tiger gurgled his disgust most plainly.

That night, Josh and I comforted ourselves, and made Dan and Willie unhappy, with tales of what we had done in the waters of the Cumberland—sixty bass in one day—four four-pounders in two hours, not to mention one little whale that drew the scales down to the five-pound notch three hours after I had him from the water. We recalled—he and I—how we had paddled, dragged, and lifted a clumsy canoe, **for four**

Blue-grass and Rhododendron

days, down the wild and beautiful Clinch (sometimes we had to go ahead and build canals through the ripples), shooting happy, blood-stirring rapids, but catching no fish, and how, down that river, we had foolishly done it again. This was the third time we had been enticed away from the Cumberland, and then and there we resolved to run after the gods of strange streams no more. Fish stories followed. Dan recalled how Cecil Rhodes got his start in South Africa, illustrating thereby the speed of the shark. Rhodes was poor, but he brought to a speculator news of the Franco-Prussian War in a London newspaper of a date five days later than the speculator's mail. The two got a corner on some commodity and made large money. Rhodes had got his paper from the belly of a shore-cast shark that had beaten the mail steamer by five round days. That was good, and Willie thereupon told a tale that he knew to be *true*.

"You know how rapidly a bass grows?"

We did not know.

"You know how a bass will use in the same hole year after year?"

That we did know.

"Well, I caught a yearling once, and I bet a man that he would grow six inches in a year. To test it, I tied a little tin whistle to his tail. A year later we

To the Breaks of Sandy

went and fished for him. The second day I caught him." Willie knocked the top-ashes from his pipe and puffed silently.

"Well?" we said.

Willie edged away out of reach, speaking softly.

"That tin whistle had grown to a fog-horn." We spared him, and he quickly turned to a poetico-scientific dissertation on birds and flowers in the Blue-grass and in the mountains, surprising us. He knew, positively, what even the great Mr. Burroughs did not seem to know a few years ago, that the shrike—the butcher-bird—impales mice as well as his feathered fellows on thorns, having found a nest in a thorn-tree up in the Blue-grass which was a ghastly, aërial, Indian-like burying-place for two mice and twenty song-sparrows. So, next day, Willie and I turned unavailingly to Melissa, whom we saw but once speeding through the weeds along the creek bank for home and, with success, to Nature; while the indefatigable Josh and Dan and Tiger whipped the all but responseless waters once more.

We reached camp at sunset—dispirited all. Tiger refused to be comforted until we turned loose two big catfish in a pool of the minnow branch and gave him permission to bring them out. With a happy wow Tiger sprang for the outsticking point of a horn and with a mad yelp sprang clear of the water. With one rub of his pricked nose against the bank, he jumped again. Wherever the surface of the water rippled, he made a dash, nosing under the grassy clumps where the fish tried to hide. Twice he got one clear of the water, but it was hard to hold to the slippery, leathery skins. In ten minutes he laid both, gasping, on the bank.

Next morning we struck camp. Willie said he would go on ahead and let down the fence—which was near Melissa's cabin. He was sitting on the fence, with a disconsolate pipe between his teeth, when we rattled and shook over the stony way up the creek—sitting alone. Yet he confessed. He had had a brief farewell with Melissa. What did she say?

"She said she was sorry we were going," said modest Willie, but he did not say what he said; and he lifted the lid of the typewriter case, the label of which was slowly emptying to a sad and empty lie.

"Thus pass the flowers," he said, with a last backward look to the log-cabin and the black-haired, blackberry-stained figure watching at the corner. "Such is life—a lick and a promise, and then no more." The wagon passed under the hill, and Melissa, the maid of the Breaks, had come and Melissa had gone forever.

To the Breaks of Sandy

Only next day, however—for such, too, is life—the aching void in Willie's imagination, and what he was pleased to call his heart, was nicely filled again.

That night we struck the confluence of Russell's Fork and the Pound, where, under wide sycamores, the meeting of swift waters had lifted from the river-beds a high breach of white sand and had considerately overspread it with piles of dry drift-wood. The place was ideal—why not try it there? The freedom of gypsies was ours, and we did. There was no rain in the sky, so we pitched no tent, but slept on the sand, under the leaves of the sycamore, and, by the light of the fire, we solaced ourselves with the cheery game of "draw." It was a happy night, in spite of Willie's disappointment with the game. He played with sorrow, and to his cost. He was accustomed to table stakes; he did not know how to act on a modest fifty-cent limit, being denied the noble privilege of "bluff."

"I was playing once with a fellow I knew slightly," he said, reminiscently and as though for self-comfort, "and with two others whom I didn't know at all. The money got down between me and one of the strangers, and when the other stranger dealt the last hand my suspicions were aroused. I picked up my hand. He had dealt me a full house—three aces and a pair. I made up my mind that he had dealt his con-

Blue-grass and Rhododendron

federate four of a kind, and do you know what I did? I discarded the pair and actually caught the remaining ace. When it came to a show-down he had four deuces. I scooped in all the gold, pushed over to my acquaintance what he had lost—in their presence—and left the table." Perhaps it was just as well that we denied Willie his own game, and thus kept him shorn of his strength.

Next day was hard, faithful, fruitless—Josh and I fishing up-stream and Dan and Willie wading down the "Pound"—and we came in at dark, each pair with a few three-quarter pound bass, only Willie having had a bigger catch. They had struck a mill, Dan said, which Willie entered—reappearing at once and silently setting his rod, and going back again, to reappear no more. Dan found him in there with his catch—a mountain maid, fairer even than Melissa, and *she was running the mill.*

Dan had hard work to get him away, but Willie came with a silent purpose that he unveiled at the camp-fire—when he put his rod together. He was done fishing for fish; the proper study of mankind being man, his proper study, next day, would be the maid of the mill, and he had forged his plan. He would hire a mule, put on jean trousers, a slouch hat, and a homespun shirt, buy a bag of corn, and go to the

To the Breaks of Sandy

mill. When that bag was ground, he would go out and buy another. All his life he had wanted to learn the milling business, and, while we fished, he would learn. But we had had enough, and were stern. We would move on from those hard-fished, fishless waters next day. In silent acquiescence Willie made for the wooden box and its fluid consolation, and when he was through with label and jug, the tale of the altered title was doubly true.

"No gal."

It takes very little to make humor in the woods.

We did move on, but so strong is hope and so powerful the ancient hunting instinct in us all, that we stopped again and fished again, with the same result, in the Pound. Something was wrong. Human effort could do no more. So, after sleep on a high hill, through a windstorm, it was home with us, and with unalterable decision this time we started, climbing hills, sliding down them, tooling around the edge of steep cliffs—sun-baked, bewhiskered, and happy, in spite of the days of hard, hard luck.

Tiger rode on the camp-chest just in front of me. Going up a hill the wagon jolted, and the dog slipped and fell between the wheels. The hind wheel, I saw, would pass over the dog's body, and if Tiger had been a child, I couldn't have been more numb with horror.

Blue-grass and Rhododendron

The wheel ran squarely over him, crushing him into the sand. The little fellow gave one short, brave, surprised yelp. Then he sprang up and trotted after us—unhurt. It was a miracle, easier to believe for the reason that that particular hind wheel was a wheel of kindly magic. Only an hour before it had run squarely over a little haversack in which were a bottle, a pipe, and other fragile things, and not a thing was broken. I do not believe it would have been possible so to arrange the contents and let the wheel run over it as harmlessly again.

Another night, another hot day, and another, and we were tooling down into the beautiful little valley, toward the sunset and "The Gap"—toward razor, bathtub, dinner, Willie's guitar and darky songs, and a sound, sweet sleep in each man's own bed—through dreams of green hills, gray walls, sharp peaks, and clear, swift waters, from which no fish flashed to seductive fly or crimson-streaked minnow. But with all the memories, no more of the Breaks for Josh or Dan or for me; and no more, doubtless, for Willie, though Melissa be there waiting for him, and though the other maid, with the light of mountain waters in her eyes, be dreaming of him at her mill.

After the gods of strange streams we would run no more.

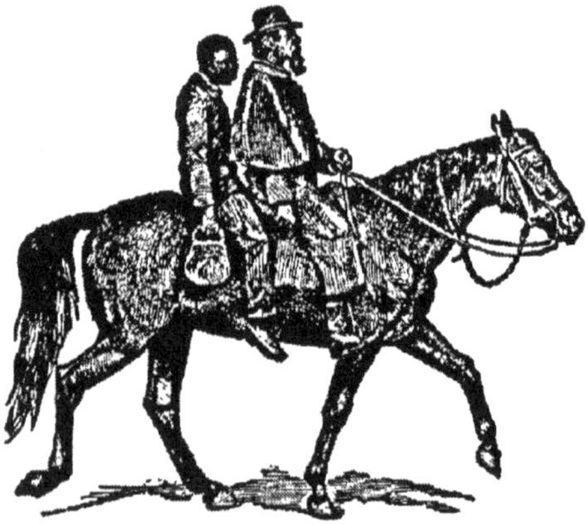

Br'er Coon in Ole Kentucky

De ole man coon am a sly ole cuss:
　　Git erlong, coon-dog, now !
An' de lady coon am a leetle bit wuss ;
　　Git erlong, coon-dog, now !

We hunts 'em when de nights gits dark ;
　　Git erlong, coon-dog, now !
Dey runs when dey hears de big dogs bark ;
　　Git erlong, coon-dog, now !

But 'deed, Mister Coon, hit's no use to try;
　　Git erlong, coon-dog, now !
Fer when we comes you's boun' to die ;
　　Git erlong, coon-dog, now !

THE day was late in autumn. The sun was low, and the haze of Indian summer hung like mist on the horizon. Crows were rising from fat pickings in the blue-grass fields, and stretching away in long lines through a yellow band of western light, and toward the cliffs of the Kentucky River, where they roost in safety the winter long. An hour later darkness fell, and we rode forth the same way, some fifty strong.

Blue-grass and Rhododendron

There were "young cap'n," as "young marster" is now called, and his sister Miriam; Northcott, who was from the North, and was my friend; young farmers from the neighborhood, with their sisters and sweethearts; a party from the county town not far away; a contingent from the Iroquois Hunt Club, of Lexington; old Tray, a tobacco tenant from the Cumberland foot-hills; and old Ash, a darky coon-hunter who is known throughout the State.

There were White Child and Black Babe, two young coon-dogs which Ash claimed as his own; Bulger, a cur that belonged to Tray; young captain's favorites, June Bug and Star; several dogs from the neighborhood; and two little fox-terriers, trotting to heel, which the Major, a veteran, had brought along to teach the country folks a new wrinkle in an old sport.

Ash was a ragged, old-time darky with a scraggly beard and a caressing voice. He rode a mule with a blind bridle and no saddle. In his belt, and hanging behind, was an ax-head fixed to a handle of hatchet length; the purpose of this was to cut a limb from under Br'er Coon when he could not be shaken off, or to cut a low entrance into his hole, so that he could be prodded out at the top with a sharp stick. In his pockets were matches to build a fire, that the fight

Br'er Coon in Ole Kentucky

could be seen; at his side hung a lantern with which
" to shine his eye " when the coon was treed; and
under him was a meal-sack for Br'er Possum.

Tobacco had brought Tray from the foot-hills to the
Blue-grass. His horse was as sorry as Ash's mule,
and he wore a rusty gray overcoat and a rusty slouch-
hat. The forefinger of his bridle-hand was off at the
second joint—a coon's teeth had nipped it as clean
as the stroke of a surgeon's knife, one night, when he
ran into a fight to pull off a young dog. Tray and
Ash betrayed a racial inheritance of mutual contempt
that was intensified by the rivalry of their dogs.
From these two, the humanity ran up, in the matter
of dress, through the young farmers and country girls,
and through the hunt club, to Northcott, who was
conventional perfection, and young captain's picturesque sister, who wore the white slouch-hat of some
young cavalryman,—the brim pinned up at the side
with the white wing of a pigeon that she had shot with
her own hand.

The cavalcade moved over the turf of the front
woods, out the pike gate, and clattered at a gallop for
two miles down the limestone road. Here old Ash
called a halt; and he and Tray, and young captain
and Blackburn, who was tall, swarthy, and typical,
rode on ahead. I was allowed to follow in order to

see the dogs work. So was Northcott; but he preferred to stay behind for a while.

"Keep back thar now," shouted Ash to the crowd, "an' keep still!" So they waited behind while we went on. The old darky threw the dogs off in a woodland to the left, and there was dead silence for a while, and the mystery of darkness. By and by came a short, eager yelp.

II

ONLY two days before, Northcott and I were down in the Kentucky mountains fishing for bass in the Cumberland, and a gaunt mountaineer was helping us catch minnows.

"Coons is a-gittin' fat," he remarked sententiously to another mountaineer, who was lazily following us up the branch; "an' they's a-gittin' fat on my corn."

"You like coons?" I asked.

"Well, jes gimme all the coon I can eat in three days—in three days, mind ye—an' then lay me up in bed ag'in a jug o' moonshine—" Words failed him there, and he waved his hand. "Them coons kin have all o' my corn they kin hold. I'd jes as lieve have my corn in coons as in a crib. I keeps my dawgs tied up so the coons kin take their time; but"—he

Br'er Coon in Ole Kentucky

turned solemnly to his companion again — "coons is a-gittin' fat, an' I'm goin' to turn them dawgs loose."

White moonshine, coons, and sweet potatoes for the Kentucky mountaineer; and on through the Bluegrass and the Purchase to the Ohio, and no farther— red whiskey, coons, and sweet potatoes for the night-roving children of Ham. It is a very old sport in the State. As far back as 1785, one shouting Methodist preacher is known to have trailed a virgin forest for old Br'er Coon. He was called Raccoon John Smith, and he is doubtless the father of the hunt in Kentucky. Traced back through Virginia, the history of the chase would most likely strike root in the homesickness of certain English colonists for trailing badgers of nights in the old country, and sending terriers into the ground for them. One night, doubtless, some man of these discovered what a plucky fight a certain ring-tailed, black-muzzled, bear-like little beast would put up at the least banter; and thereafter, doubtless, every man who loved to hunt the badger was ready to hunt the coon. That is the theory of a distinguished Maryland lawyer and coon-hunter, at least, and it is worthy of record. The sport is common in Pennsylvania, and also in Connecticut, where the hunters finish the coon with a shot-gun; and in New

Blue-grass and Rhododendron

England, I am told, " drawing " the coon is yet done. Br'er Coon is placed in a long, square box or trough, and the point is to get a fox-terrier that is game enough to go in " and bring him out." That, too, is an inheritance from the English way of badger-fighting, which was tried on our American badgers without success, as it was usually found necessary, after a short fight, to draw out the terrier—dead. Coon-hunting is, however, distinctly a Southern sport, although the coon is found all over the United States, and as far north as Alaska. It is the darky who has made the sport Southern. With him it has always been, is now, and always will be, a passion. Inseparable are the darky and his coon-dog. And nowhere in the South is the sport more popular than in Kentucky—with mountaineers, negroes, and people of the Blue-grass. It is the more remarkable, then, that of all the beasts that walk the blue-grass fields, the coon-dog is the only one for which the Kentuckian does not claim superiority. The Kentucky coon-dog—let his master get full credit for the generous concession—is no better than the coon-dog of any other State. Perhaps this surprising apathy is due to the fact that the coon-dog has no family position. A prize was offered in 1891 by the Blue-grass Kennel Club at Lexington, and was won, of course, by a Kentucky dog; but the

Br'er Coon in Ole Kentucky

American Kennel Club objected, and the prize has never been offered again. So the coon-dog has no recognized breed. He is not even called a hound. He is a dog—just a "dawg." He may be cur, fox-terrier, fox-hound, or he may have all kinds of grand-parents. On one occasion that is worth interjecting he was even a mastiff. An Irishman in Louisville owned what he called the "brag coon-dog" of the State. There are big woods near Louisville, and a good deal of hunting for the coon is done in them. A German who lived in the same street had a mastiff with the playful habit of tossing every cat that came into his yard over the fence—dead. The Irishman conceived the idea that the mastiff would make the finest coon-dog on earth—not excepting his own. He persuaded the German to go out in the woods with him one night, and he took his own dog along to teach the mastiff how to fight. The coon was shaken out of the tree. The coon-dog made for the coon, and the mastiff made for the coon-dog, and reached him before he reached the coon. In a minute the coon-dog was dead, the coon was making off through the rustling maize, and Celt and Teuton were clinched under the spreading oak. Originally, the coon-dog was an uncompromising cur, or a worthless fox-hound that had dropped out of his pack; and most likely darkies and boys had a monopoly of the sport in the good old days when the hunting was purely for the fun of the fight, and when trees were cut down, and nobody took the trouble to climb. When the red fox drove out the gray, the newer and swifter hounds—old Lead's descendants—took away the occupation of the old fox-hound, and he, in turn, took the place of the cur; so that the Kentucky coon-dog of to-day is usually the old-fashioned hound that was used to hunt the gray fox, the " pot-licker "—the black-and-tan, long-eared, rat-tailed, flat-bellied, splay-footed " pot-licker." Such a hound is a good trailer; he makes a good fight, and there is no need in the hunt for special speed. Recently the terrier has been introduced to do the fighting when the coon has been trailed and treed, because he is a more even match, and as game as any dog; and, thanks to Mr. Belmont's " Nursery " in the Blue-grass, the best terriers are accessible to the Kentucky hunters who want that kind of fight.

But it is the hunt with an old darky, and old coon-dogs, and a still, damp, dark night, that is dear to the Southern hunter's heart. It is the music of the dogs, the rivalry between them, the subtleties of the trail, and the quick, fierce fight, that give the joy then. Only recently have the ladies begun to take part in the sport, and, naturally, it is growing in favor. Coons

Br'er Coon in Ole Kentucky

are plentiful in the Blue-grass, even around the towns, where truck-patches are convenient, and young turkeys and chickens unwary. For a coon, unless hard-pressed, will never go up any tree but his own; and up his own tree he is usually safe, for trees are now too valuable to be cut down for coons.

It is the ride of only a few hours from the mountains to the lowland Blue-grass, and down there, too, coons were getting fat; so on the morning of the second day Northcott and I woke up in the ell of an old-fashioned Blue-grass homestead—an ell that was known as the "office" in slavery days—and old Ash's gray head was thrust through the open door.

"Breakfast 'mos' ready. Young cap'n say you mus' git up now."

Crackling flames were leaping up the big chimney from the ash kindling-wood and hickory logs piled in the enormous fireplace, and Northcott, from his bed in the corner, chuckled with delight.

That morning the Northerner rode through peaceful fields and woodlands, and looked at short-horn cattle and Southdown sheep and thorough-bred horses, and saw the havoc that tobacco was bringing to the lovely land. When he came back dinner was ready— his first Southern dinner.

Blue-grass and Rhododendron

After dinner, Miriam took him to feed young captain's pet coon, the Governor, and Black Eye, a fox-terrier that was the Governor's best friend—both in the same plate. The Governor was chained to an old apple-tree, and slept in a hole which he had enlarged for himself about six feet from the ground. Let a strange dog appear, and the Governor would retreat, and Black Eye attack; and after the fight the Governor would descend, and plainly manifest his gratitude with slaps and scratches and bites of tenderness. The Governor never looked for anything that was tossed him, but would feel for it with his paws, never lowering his blinking eyes at all. Moreover, he was a dainty beast, for he washed everything in a basin of water before he ate it.

"Dey eats ever'thing, boss," said old Ash's soft voice; "but dey likes crawfish best. I reckon coon 'll eat dawg, jes as dawg eats coon. But dawg won't eat 'possum. Gib a dawg a piece o' 'possum meat, and he spit it out, and look at you mean and reproachful. Knowin' 'possum lack I do, dat sut'nly do look strange. Hit do, mon, shore.

"An' as fer fightin'—well, I ain't never seed a coon dat wouldn't fight, an' I ain't never seed nuttin' dat a coon wouldn't tackle. Most folks believes dat a 'possum *can't* fight. Well, you jes tie a 'possum an'

Br'er Coon in Ole Kentucky

coon together by de tails, an' swing 'em over a clothes-line, an' when you come back you gwine find de coon daid. 'Possum jes take hole in de throat, an' go to sleep—jes like a bull-pup."

A gaunt figure in a slouch-hat and ragged overcoat had slouched in at the yard gate. His eye was blue and mild, and his face was thin and melancholy. Old Ash spoke to him familiarly, and young captain called him Tray. He had come for no reason other than that he was mildly curious and friendly; and he stopped shyly behind young captain, fumbling with the stump of one finger at a little sliver of wood that served as the one button to his overcoat, silent, listless, gentle, grave. And there the three stood, the pillars of the old social structure that the war brought down —the slave, the poor white, the master of one and the lord of both. Between one and the other the chasm was still deep, but they would stand shoulder to shoulder in the hunt that night.

"Dat wind from de souf," said old Ash, as we turned back to the house. "Git cloudy bime-by. We gwine to git Mister Coon dis night, shore."

A horn sounded from the quarters soon after supper, and the baying of dogs began. Several halloos came through the front woods, and soon there was the stamping of horses' feet about the yard fence, and much jolly laughter. Girths were tightened, and a little later the loud slam of the pike gate announced that the hunt was begun.

III

> Br'er Coon he has a bushy tail;
> Br'er Possum's tail am bar';
> Br'er Rabbit's got no tail at all—
> Jes a leetle bunch o' ha'r.

WHEN the yelp came, Tray's lips opened triumphantly:

"Bulger!"

"Rabbit," said old Ash, contemptuously.

Bulger was a young dog, and only half broken; but every hunter knew that each old dog had stopped in his tracks and was listening. There was another yelp and another; and the old dogs harked to him. But the hunters sat still to give the dogs time to trail, as hunters always do. Sometimes they will not move for half an hour, unless the dogs are going out of hearing. Old Ash was humming calmly:

> Coony in de tree;
> 'Possum in de holler;
> Purty gal at my house,
> Fat as she kin waller.

Br'er Coon in Ole Kentucky

It was Tray's dog, and old Ash could afford to be calm and scornful, for he was without faith. So over and over he sang it softly, while Tray's mouth was open, and his ear was eagerly cocked to every note of the trail. The air was very chilly and damp. The moon was no more than a silver blotch in a leaden sky, and barely visible here and there was a dim star. On every side, the fields and dark patches of woodland rolled alike to the horizon, except straight ahead, where one black line traced the looping course of the river. That way the dogs were running, and the music was growing furious. It was too much for Tray, who suddenly let out the most remarkable yell I have ever heard from human lips. That was a signal to the crowd behind. A rumbling started; the crowd was striking the hard turnpike at a swift gallop, coming on. It was quick work for Bulger, and the melancholy of Tray's face passed from under the eager light in his eyes, and as suddenly came back like a shadow. The music had stopped short, and old Ash pulled in with a grunt of disgust.

"Rabbit, I tol' ye," he said again, contemptuously; and Tray looked grieved. A dog with a strange mouth gave tongue across the dim fields.

"House cat," said young captain. "That was a farm dog. The young dogs ran the cat home." This was true, for just then two of the old dogs leaped the fence and crossed the road.

"They won't hark to him next time," said young captain; "Bulger's a liar." A coon-dog is never worthless, "no 'count;" he is simply a "liar." Nine out of ten young dogs will run a rabbit or a house cat. The old dogs will trust a young one once or twice; but if he proves unworthy of confidence, they will not go to him sometimes when he is really on a coon trail, and will have to be called by their masters after the coon is treed. As Bulger sprang into the road, old Ash objurgated him:

"Whut you mean, dawg?—you black liah, you!"

The pain in Tray's face was pathetic.

"Bulger hain't no liar," he said sturdily. "Bulger's jes young."

Then we swept down the road another mile to another woodland, and this time I stayed with the crowd behind. Young captain had given Northcott his favorite saddle-horse and a fat saddle that belonged to his father; and Northcott, though a cross-country rider at home, was not happy. He was being gently rocked sidewise in a maddening little pace that made him look as ridiculous as he felt.

"You haven't ridden a Southern saddle-horse before, have you?" said Miriam.

Br'er Coon in Ole Kentucky

"No; I never have."

"Then you won't mind a few instructions?"

"No, indeed," he said meekly.

"Well, press your hand at the base of his neck—so—and tighten your reins just a little—now."

The horse broke step into a "running walk," which was a new sensation to Northcott. We started up the pace a little.

"Now press behind your saddle on the right side, and tighten your rein a little more, and hold it steady —so—and he'll rack." The saddler struck a swift gait that was a revelation to the Northerner.

"Now, if you want him to trot, catch him by the mane or by the right ear."

The horse broke his step instantly.

"Beautiful!" said Northcott. "This is my gait."

"Now wave your hand—so." The animal struck an easy lope.

"Lovely!"

We swept on. A young countryman who was called Tom watched the instruction with provincial amusement.

I was riding young captain's buggy mare, and, trying her over a log, I learned that she could jump. So, later in the night, I changed horses with Northcott— for a purpose.

Blue-grass and Rhododendron

We could hear the dogs trailing around to the right now, and the still figures of Ash and Tray halted us in the road. Presently the yelps fused into a musical chorus, and then a long, penetrating howl came through the woods that was eloquent to the knowing.

"Dar's old Star," said Ash, kicking his mule in the side; "an' dar's a coon!"

We had a dash through the woods at a gallop then, and there was much dodging of low branches, and whisking around tree-trunks, and a great snapping of brush on the ground; and we swept out of the shadows of the woodland to a white patch of moonlight, in the centre of which was a little walnut-tree. About this the dogs were sitting on their haunches, baying up at its leafless branches; and there, on the first low limb, scarcely ten feet from the ground and two feet from the trunk, sat, not ring-tailed Br'er Coon, but a fat, round, gray 'possum, paying no attention at all to the hunters gathering under him, but keeping each of his beady black eyes moving with nervous quickness from one dog to another. Old Ash was laughing triumphantly in the rear. "Black Babe foun' dat 'possum. Dis nigger's got dawgs!" Northcott was called up, that he might see; and young captain rode under the little fellow, and, reaching up, caught him by the tail, the 'possum making no effort at all to escape, so en-

Br'er Coon in Ole Kentucky

grossed was he with the dogs. Old Ash, with a wide smile, dropped him into the mouth of his meal-sack.

"Won't he smother in there," asked Northcott, "or eat his way out?"

Old Ash grinned. "He'll be dar when we git home." Then he turned to Tray. "I gwine to let you have dis 'possum in de morning, to train dat liah Bulger."

There is no better way to train a young dog than to let him worry a 'possum after he has found it; and this is not as cruel as it seems. Br'er 'Possum knows how to roll up in a ball and protect his vitals; and when you think he is about dead, he will unroll, but little hurt.

The clouds were breaking now; the moon showed full, the air had grown crisp, and the stars were thick and brilliant. For half an hour we sat on a hill-side waiting, and, for some occult reason, the Major was becoming voluble.

"Now, old Tray there thinks he's hunting the coon. So does old Ash. I reckon that we are all laboring under that painful delusion. Whereas the truth is that the object of this hunt is attained. I refer, sir, to that 'possum." He turned to Northcott. "You have never eaten 'possum? Well, sir, it is a very easy and dangerous habit to contract if the 'possum is properly prepared. I venture to say, sir, that nawth of Mason and Dixon's line the gastronomical possibilities of the 'possum are utterly unknown. How do I prepare him? Well, sir——"

The Major was interrupted by a mighty yell from old Ash; and again there was a great rush through the low undergrowth, over the rocky hill-side, and down a long, wooded hollow. This time the old negro's favorites, White Child and Black Babe, were in the lead; and old Ash flapped along like a windmill, with every tooth in sight.

"Go it, Black Babe! Go it, my White Chile! Gord! but dis nigger's got *dawgs!*"

Everybody caught his enthusiasm, and we could hear the crowd thundering behind us. I was next Ash, and all of a sudden the old darky came to a quick stop, and caught at his nose with one hand. A powerful odor ran like an electric shock through the air, and a long howl from each dog told that each had started from some central point on his own responsibility. The Major raised his voice. "Stop!" he shouted. "Keep the ladies back—keep 'em *'way* back!"

"Gord!" said old Ash once more; and Tray lay down on his horse's neck, helpless with laughter.

The Major was too disgusted for words. When

"Go it, Black Babe! Go it, my White Chile!"

Br'er Coon in Ole Kentucky

we crossed the road, and paused again, he called in a loud voice for me to advance and see the dogs work. Then he directed me to call Northcott forward for the same purpose. Blackburn came, too. A moment later I heard young captain shouting to the crowd, "Keep back, keep back!" and he, too, spurred around the bushes.

"Where are those dogs?" he asked with mock anxiety.

The neck of the Major's horse was lengthened peacefully through the rails of a ten-foot fence, and at the question the veteran whisked a bottle of old Jordan from his hip.

"Here they are."

Then followed an eloquent silence that turned the cold October air into the night-breath of June, that made the mists warm, the stars rock, and the moon smile. Once more we waited.

"How do I prepare him, sir?" said the Major. "You skin the coon; but you singe off the hair of the 'possum in hot wood-ashes, because the skin is a delicacy, and must not be scalded. Then parbile him. This takes a certain strength away, and makes him more tender. Then put him in a pan, with a good deal of butter, pepper, and salt, and a little brown flour, leaving the head and tail on. Then cut little slips along the ribs and haunches, and fill them with red-pepper pods. Baste him with gravy while browning "—the Major's eyes brightened, and once at least his lips smacked distinctly—" cook sweet potatoes around him, and then serve him smoking hot—though some, to be sure, prefer him cold, like roast pork. You must have dodgers, very brown and very crisp; and, of course, raw persimmons (persimmons are ripe in 'possum-time, and 'possums like persimmons—the two are inseparable); pickles, chow-chow, and tomato ketchup; and, lastly, pumpkin-pie and a second cup of coffee. Then, with a darky and a banjo, a mint-julep and a pipe, you may have a reasonable expectation of being, for a little while, happy. And speaking of julep——"

Just then two dim forms were moving out of sight behind some bushes below us, and the Major shouted:

"Tawm!"

The two horsemen turned reluctantly, and when Tom was near enough the Major asked a whispered question, and got an affirmative response.

"All right," added the Major, with satisfaction. "Shake hands with Mr. Northcott. I hereby promote you, sir, to the privilege of staying in front and watching the dogs work."

Northcott's face was distinctly flushed after this

Br'er Coon in Ole Kentucky

promotion, and he confessed afterward to an insane desire to imitate the Major's speech and Blackburn's stately manner. When we started off again, he posted along with careless content, and many sympathized with him.

"Oh, this is just what I like," he said. "Everybody posts up North—even the ladies."

"Dear me!" said several.

"I reckon that kind of a horse is rather better for an inexperienced rider," said Tom, friendly, and Northcott smiled. Somebody tried a horse over a log a few minutes later, and the horse swerved to one side. Northcott wheeled, and started for a bigger log at a gallop; and the little mare rose, as if on wings, two feet higher than was necessary, while Northcott sat as if bound to his saddle.

Then he leaped recklessly into another field, and back again. Tom was speechless.

It was after midnight now, and the moon and stars were passing swiftly overhead; but the crowd started with undiminished enthusiasm when a long howl announced that some dog had treed. This time it was no mistake. At the edge of the woodland sat the old darky at the foot of the tree to keep the coon from coming down, while the young dogs were bouncing madly about him, and baying up into the tree. It was

Blue-grass and Rhododendron

curious to watch old Star when he arrived. He would take no pup's word for the truth, but circled the tree to find out whether the coon had simply " marked " it; and, satisfied on that point, he settled down on his haunches, and, with uplifted muzzle, bayed with the rest.

"I knowed dis was coon," said Ash, rising. "'Possum circles; coon runs straight."

Then the horses were tied, and everybody gathered twigs and branches and dead wood for a fire, which was built half-way between the trunk and the tips of the overhanging branches; and old Ash took off his shoes, his coat, and his " vest," for no matter how cold the night, the darky will climb in shirt, socks, and trousers. If he can reach around the tree, he will go up like a monkey; if he can't, he will go to the outer edge, and pull a bough down. In this case he could do neither, so young captain stood with his hands braced against the tree, while the old darky climbed up his back, and stamped in sock feet over his head and shoulders. Tray held the fence-rail alongside, and, with the aid of this, the two boosted Ash to the first limb. Then the men formed a circle around the tree at equal distances, each man squatting on the ground, and with a dog between his knees. The Major held his terriers; and as everybody had seen the

Br'er Coon in Ole Kentucky

usual coon-fight, it was agreed that the terriers should have the first chance. Another darky took a lantern, and walked around the tree with the lantern held just behind one ear, " to shine the coon's eye." As the lantern is moved around, the coon's eye follows, and its greenish-yellow glow betrays his whereabouts.

" Dar he is! " shouted the negro with the lantern; " 'way up higher." And there he was, on the extremity of a long limb. Old Ash climbed slowly until he could stand on the branch below and seize with both hands the limb that the coon lay on.

" Look out dar, now; hyeh he comes! " Below, everybody kept perfectly quiet, so that the dogs could hear the coon strike the ground if he should sail over their heads and light in the darkness outside the circle of fire. Ash shook, the coon dropped straight, and the game little terriers leaped for him. Br'er Coon turned on his back, and it was slap, bite, scratch, and tear. One little terrier was caught in the nose and spun around like a top, howling; but he went at it again. For a few minutes there was an inextricable confusion of a brown body, snapping white teeth, and outshooting claws, with snarling, leaping little black-and-tan terriers, and much low, fierce snarling. The coon's wheezing snarl was curious: it had rage, whining terror, and perfect courage, all in one. Then came one scream, penetrating and piteous, and the fight was done.

"Git him?" yelled Ash from up in the tree.

"Yep."

"Well, dar's anudder one up hyeh. Watch out, now!"

The branches rattled, but no coon dropped, and we could hear Ash muttering high in the air, "I bet ef I had a black-snake whip I'd lif' you."

Then came a pistol-shot. Ash had fired close to him to make him jump; but Br'er Coon lay close to the limb, motionless.

"I got to cut him off, I reckon," Ash called; and whack! whack! went the blows of his little ax. "Whoop!"

The branch crackled; a dark body, flattened, and with four feet outstretched, came sailing down, and struck the earth—thud! Every dog leaped for him, growling; every man yelled, and pressed close about the heap of writhing bodies; and there was pandemonium. A coon can fight eight dogs better than he can fight three, for the eight get in one another's way. Foot by foot the game little beast fought his way to the edge of the cliff, and the whole struggling, snarling, snapping mass rolled, with dislodged dirt and clattering stones, down to the edge of the river, with

Br'er Coon in Ole Kentucky

the yelling hunters slipping and sliding after them. A great splash followed, and then a sudden stillness. One dog followed the coon into the water, and after a sharp struggle, and a howl of pain, turned and made for the bank. It was Bulger—the last to give up the fight. Br'er Coon had escaped, and there was hardly a man who was not glad.

"Reckon Bulger can fight, ef he is a liar," said Tray—"which he ain't."

The stars were sinking fast, and we had been five hours in the saddle. Everybody was tired. Down in a ravine young captain called a halt when the dogs failed to strike another trail. The horses were tied, and an enormous fire was built, and everybody gathered in a great circle around it. Somebody started a song, and there was a jolly chorus. A little piccaninny was pushed into the light, bashful and hesitating.

"Shake yo' foot, boy," said old Ash, sternly; and the nimble feet were shaken to "Juba" and "My Baby Loves Shortenin'-bread." It was a scene worth remembering—the upshooting flames, the giant shadows leaping into the dark woods about, the circle of young girls with flushed faces and loosened hair, and strapping young fellows cracking jokes, singing songs, and telling stories.

Blue-grass and Rhododendron

It was all simple and genuine, and it pleased Northcott, who was one of the many Northerners to whom everything Southern appeals strongly—who had come South prepared to like everything Southern: darkies, darky songs; Southern girls, Southern songs, old-fashioned in tune and sentiment; Southern voices, Southern accent, Southern ways; the romance of the life and the people; the pathos of the war and its ruins; the simple, kindly hospitality of the Southern home.

Nobody noticed that Tray was gone, and nobody but Tray had noticed that Bulger was the only one of the dogs that had not gathered in to the winding of old Ash's horn. A long howl high on the cliff made known the absence of both. It was Bulger; and again came Tray's remarkable yell. Not an old dog moved. Again came the howl, and again the yell; and then Tray was silent, though the howls went on. Another song was started, and stopped by old Ash, who sprang to his feet. A terrific fight was going on up on the cliff. We could hear Bulger's growl, the unmistakable snarl of a coon, a series of cheering yells, and the cracking of branches, as though Tray were tumbling out of a tree. Every dog leaped from the fire, and all the darkies but old Ash leaped after them. There was a scramble up the cliff; and ten minutes later Tray came into the firelight with a coon in one hand, and

Br'er Coon in Ole Kentucky

poor Bulger limping after him, bleeding at the throat, and with a long, bloody scratch down his belly.

"Bulger treed him, an' I seed the coon 'twixt me an' the moon. I hollered fer you, an' you wouldn't come, so I climbed up an' shuk him out. When I got down the coon was dead. Bulger don't run polecats," he said with mild scorn, and turned on Ash: "I reckon you'd better not call Bulger a liar no more." And the blood of the Anglo-Saxon told, for Ash made no answer.

It was toward morning now. Only one white star was hanging where the rest had gone down. There was a last chorus—"My Old Kentucky Home":

We'll hunt no more for the 'possum an' the coon.

And then, at a swift gallop, we thundered ten miles along the turnpike—home. The crowd fell away, and day broke as we neared young captain's roof. The crows were flying back from the cliffs to the bluegrass fields, and the first red light of the sun was shooting up the horizon. Northcott was lifting Miriam from her saddle as I rode into the woods; and when I reached the yard fence they were seated on the porch, as though they meant to wait for the sunrise. At the foot of the apple-tree were the Governor and Black Eye, playing together like kittens.

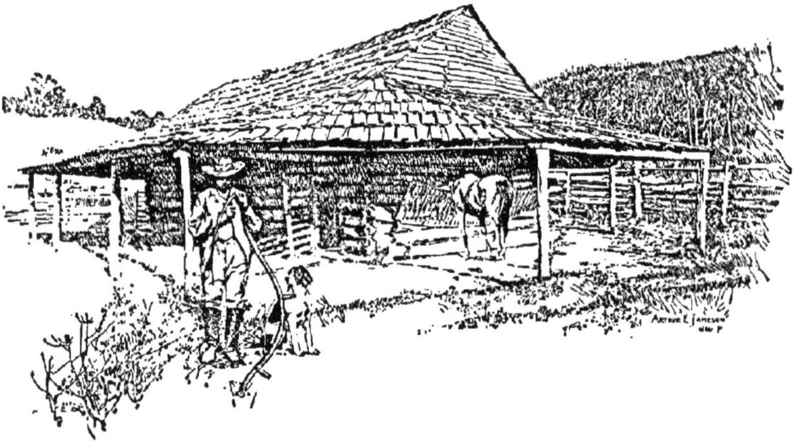

Civilizing the Cumberland

HALF a century ago the Southern mountaineer was what he is now, in the main—truthful, honest, courageous, hospitable—and more: he was peaceable and a man of law. During the last fifteen years, fact and fiction have made his lawlessness broadly known; and yet, in spite of his moonshining, his land-thieving, and his feuds, I venture the paradox that he still has at heart a vast respect for the law; and that, but for the war that put weapons in his Anglo-Saxon fists, murder in his heart, and left him in his old isolation; but for the curse of the revenue service that criminalizes the innocent, and the system of land laws that sometimes makes it necessary for the mountaineer of Kentucky and Virginia, at least, to practically steal his own home—he would be a law-abiding citizen to-day. But he is not law-abiding, and, therefore, the caption above these words.

Of course, the railroad comes first as an element of civilization; but unless the church and the school, in

Blue-grass and Rhododendron

the ratio of several schools to each church, quickly follow, the railroad does the mountaineer little else than great harm. Even with the aid of these three, the standards of conduct of the outer world are reared slowly. A painful process of evolution has been the history of every little mountain-town that survived the remarkable mushroom growth which, within the year of 1889-90, ran from Pennsylvania to Alabama along both bases of the Cumberland. With one vivid exception: in one of these towns, civilization forged ahead of church, school, and railroad. The sternest ideals of good order and law were set up at once and maintained with Winchester, pistol, policeman's billy, and whistle. It was a unique experiment in civilization, and may prove of value to the lawful among the lawless elsewhere; and the means to the end were unique.

In this town, certain young men—chiefly Virginians and blue-grass Kentuckians—simply formed a volunteer police-guard. They enrolled themselves as county policemen, and each man armed himself—usually with a Winchester, a revolver, a billy, a belt, a badge, and a whistle—a most important detail of the accoutrement, since it was used to call for help. They were lawyers, bankers, real-estate brokers, newspaper men, civil and mining engineers, geologists,

Civilizing the Cumberland

speculators, and several men of leisure. Nearly all were in active business—as long as there was business—and most of them were college graduates, representing Harvard, Yale, Princeton, the University of Virginia, and other Southern colleges. Two were great-grandsons of Henry Clay, several bore a like relation to Kentucky governors, and, with few exceptions, the guard represented the best people of the blue-grass of one State and the tide-water country of the other. All served without pay, of course, and, in other words, it was practically a police-force of gentlemen who did the rough, every-day work of policemen, without swerving a hair's-breadth from the plain line of the law. These young fellows guarded the streets, day and night, when there was need; they made arrests, chased and searched for criminals, guarded jails against mobs, cracked toughs over the head with billies, lugged them to the "calaboose," and appeared as witnesses against them in court next morning. They drilled faithfully, and such was the discipline that a whistle blown at any hour of day or night would bring a dozen armed men to the spot in half as many minutes. In time, a drunken man was a rare sight on the streets; the quiet was rarely disturbed by a disorderly yell or a pistol-shot, and I have seen a crowd of mountaineers, wildly hilarious and flourishing bottles and pistols as they

Blue-grass and Rhododendron

came in from the hills, take on the meekness of lambs when they crossed the limits of that little mountain-town. I do not believe better order was kept anywhere in the land. It was, perhaps, the only mountain-town along the border where a feud, or a street fight of more than ten minutes' duration, was impossible. Being county policemen, the guards extended their operations to the limits of the county, thirty miles away, and in time created a public sentiment fearless enough to convict a certain desperado of murder; then each man left his business and, in a body, the force went to the county-seat, twenty miles away, and stayed there for a month to guard the condemned man and prevent his clan from rescuing him—thus making possible the first hanging that ever took place in that region. Later, they maintained a fund for the proper prosecution of criminals, and I believe that any man in the county, if guilty of manslaughter, would have selected any spot south of Mason and Dixon's line other than his own county-seat for his trial. Indeed, the enthusiasm for the law was curiously contagious. Wild fellows, who would have been desperadoes themselves but for the vent that enforcing the law gave to their energies, became the most enthusiastic members of the guard. In other parts of the county, natives formed similar bands and searched for outlaws. Sim-

Civilizing the Cumberland

ilar organizations were formed in other " boom " towns round about; so that over in the Kentucky mountains, a hundred miles away, there is to-day another volunteer police-guard at the seat of what was perhaps the most lawless county in the State, and once the seat of a desperate feud. This was formed at the suggestion of one of our own men, a young and well-known geologist. So that, at that time, it looked as though the force that might one day put down lawlessness in the Southern mountains was getting its impulse from the nerve, good sense, and public spirit of two or three young bluegrass Kentuckians who had gone over into the mountains of Virginia to make their fortunes from iron, coal, and law.

For all this happened at " the Gap," which is down in the southwestern corner of old Virginia, and about eight miles from the Kentucky line. There Powell's Mountain runs its mighty ribs into the Cumberland range with such humiliating violence that the Cumberland, turned feet over head by the shock, has meekly given up its proud title and suffered somebody to dub it plain Stone Mountain; and plain Stone Mountain it is to-day—down sixty miles to Cumberland Gap. At the point of contact and from the bases of both ranges, Powell's Valley starts on its rolling way southward. Ten miles below, Roaring Fork has worn down to water-level a wild cleft through Stone Mountain and into the valley; and the torrent is still lashing the yielding feet of great cliffs and tumbling past ravines that are dark in winter with the evergreen of laurel and rhododendron, and lighted in summer with the bloom.

On the other side, South Fork drops seven hundred feet of waterfalls from Thunderstruck Knob, and the two streams sweep toward each other like the neck of a lute and, like a lute, curve away again, to come together at last and bear the noble melody of Powell's River down the valley. The neck is not over two hundred yards wide, and, in the heartlike peninsula and from ten to twenty feet above the running streams, is the town—all straightaway, but for the beautiful rise of Poplar Hill, which sinks slowly to a level again.

All this—cleft, river, and little town—is known far and wide as "the Gap." Through the Gap and on the north side of Stone Mountain, are rich veins of pure coking coal and not an ounce of iron ore; to the south is plenty of good ore and not an ounce of coal; the cliffs between are limestone; and water—the third essential to the making of iron—runs like a mill-race between. This juxtaposition of such raw materials brought in the outside world. Nearly twenty years ago, a wise old Pennsylvanian bought an empire of coal and tim-

Civilizing the Cumberland

ber-land through the Gap. Ten years ago the shadow of the "boom" started southward—for the boom is a shadow, and whatever of light there be in it is as a flash of lightning, and with a wake hardly less destructive. The Gap was strategic, and there was no such site for a town in a radius of a hundred miles. Twelve railroads were surveyed to the point, and in poured the outside world to make the town—civil and mining engineers, surveyors, coal operators, shrewd investors, reckless speculators, land-sharks; lawyers, doctors, store-keepers, real-estate agents; curb-stone brokers, saloon-keepers, gamblers, card-sharps, railroad hands—all the flotsam and jetsam of the terrible boom.

The Kentuckians came first, and two young lawyers—Logan and Macfarlan I shall call them—blazed the way; one, for the same reason, perhaps, that led his forefather, Henry Clay, to Kentucky; the other, who was of a race of pioneers, Indian-fighters, lawyers, and statesmen, because he was, in a measure, a reversal to the first ancestor who penetrated the Western wilderness. Indeed they and the young Kentuckians, who came after them, took the same trail that their fathers had taken from Virginia—going to make their fortunes from lands that the pioneers had passed over as worthless. It was these two young men who took the helm of affairs and ran the town—as a steersman

Blue-grass and Rhododendron

runs a ship—into the calm waters of good order and law.

It was quiet enough in the beginning, for, besides the cottage set in rhododendron-bushes along the deep bank of South Fork—and turned into a lawyer's office—there was only a blacksmith's shop, one store, one farm-house, and a little frame hotel—"The Grand Central Hotel." But, for half a century, the Gap had been the chief voting-place in the district. Here were the muster-days of war-times, and at the mouth of the Gap camped Captain Mayhall Wells and his famous Army of the Callahan. Here was the only store, the only grist-mill, the only woollen-mill, in the region. The Gap was, in consequence, the chief gathering-place of people for miles around. Here in the old days met the bullies of neighboring counties, and here was fought a famous battle between a famous bully of Wise and a famous bully of Lee. Only, in those days, the men fought with nature's weapons—with all of them—and, after the fight, got up and shook hands. Here, too, was engendered the hostility between the hill-dwellers of Wise and the valley men of Lee; so that the Gap had ever been characterized by a fine spirit of personal liberty, and any wild oats that were not sown elsewhere in that region, usually sprouted at the Gap. So, too, when the boom started, the new-

Civilizing the Cumberland

comers, disliked on their own account as interlopers, shared this local hostility, which got expression usually on Saturday afternoons in the exhilaration of moonshine, much yelling and shooting and bantering, an occasional fist-fight, and, sometimes, in a usually harmless interchange of shots. But it was the mountain-brother who gave the Kentuckians most trouble at first. Sometimes the Kentucky feudsmen would chase each other over Black Mountain and into the Gap. Sometimes a band of them on horseback— "wild jayhawkers from old Kanetuck," they used to be called—would be passing through to "Commencement" at a mountain-college down the valley, and there would be high jinks indeed. They would halt at the Gap and "load up," as the phrase was—with moonshine; usually it was a process of reloading. Then they would race their horses up and down the street.

Sometimes they would quite take the town, and the store-keepers would close up and go to the woods to wait for the festivities to come to a natural end. This was endured because it was only periodical, and because, apparently, it couldn't be cured.

Later on, after the speculators had pooled their lands and laid out the coming town, and the human stream began to trickle in from the outer world, an enterpris-

Blue-grass and Rhododendron

ing Hoosier came in and established a brick-plant. He employed a crowd of Tennessee mountaineers, who worked with their pistols buckled around them. By and by came a strike, and, that night, the hands shot out the lights and punctured the chromos in the boarding-house. Then they got sticks, clubs, knives, and pistols, and marched up through town, intimidating and threatening.

Verbal, the town constable, tackled one of them valiantly, shouting at the same time for help. For ten minutes he shouted and fought, and then, once again, his voice rose: " I've fit an' I've hollered fer help," he cried, " an' I've hollered fer help an' I've fit—an' I've fit agin. Now this town can go to h—l." And he tore off his badge and threw it on the ground, and went off, weeping.

Next morning, which was Sunday, the brick-yard gang took another triumphant march through town, and when they went back, Logan and Macfarlan, his partner, called for volunteers to go down and put the whole crowd under arrest. To Logan's disgust, only a few seemed willing to go, but when the few, who would go, started, Logan, leading them, looked back from the top of Poplar Hill, and the whole town seemed to be strung out behind him. Below the hill, he saw the toughs drawn up in two bodies for battle,

Civilizing the Cumberland

and, as he led the young fellows toward them, the Hoosier rode out at a gallop, waving his hands and beside himself with anxiety and terror.

"Don't! don't!" he shouted. "Somebody'll get killed. Wait—they'll give up!" So Logan halted and the Hoosier rode back. After a short parley, he came up to say that the strikers would give up, and when Logan started again, one party dropped their clubs, put up their weapons, and sullenly waited, but the rest broke and ran. Logan ordered a pursuit, but only three or four were captured. That night the Hoosier was delirious over his troubles, and, next day, he left orders with his foreman to close down the plant, and rode off to await the passing of the storm. But the incident started the idea of a volunteer police-guard in Logan's head. A few days later it took definite shape. Constable Verbal had resigned; he had been tired for some time, and wholly inefficient, for when he arrested an outsider, the prisoner's companions would calmly rescue him and take him home; so that the calaboose—as we called the log-cabin jail, weakly stockaded and with a thin-walled guard-room adjoining—was steadily as empty as a gourd.

A few nights later, trouble came up in the chief store of the town. Two knives and two pistols were whipped out, and the proprietor blew out the light and astutely got under the counter. When the combatants scrambled outside, he locked the door and crawled out the back window. The next morning a courageous, powerful fellow named Youell took up Verbal's badge and his office, and that afternoon he had some professional service to perform in the same store. A local tough was disorderly, and Youell warned him.

"You can't arrest me," said the fellow, with an oath, but before his lips closed, Youell had him by the collar. His friends drew up in a line and threatened to kill the constable if he went through. Youell had not spoken a word and, without a word now, he pushed through, hauling his man after him.

The friends followed close with knives and pistols drawn, cursing and swearing that the man should not be jailed. The constable was white, silent, and firm, but he had to stop in front of the little law office where Logan happened to be looking out of the window. Logan went to the door.

"Look here, boys," he said, quietly, and with the tone of the peacemaker, "let's not have any row. Let him go on to the Mayor's office. If he isn't guilty, the Mayor will let him go; and if he is, the Mayor will let him give bond. There's no use having a row. Let him go on."

Now Logan, to the casual eye, appeared no more

Civilizing the Cumberland

than the ordinary man, and even a close observer would have seen no more than that his face was thoughtful, that his eye was blue and singularly clear and fearless, and that he was calm with a calmness that might come from anything else than stolidity of temperament—and that, by the way, is the self-control which counts most against the unruly passions of other men—but anybody near Logan, at a time when excitement was high and a crisis was imminent, would have felt the resultant of forces emanating from the man, that were beyond analysis.

I have known one other man—his partner, Macfarlan—to possess an even finer quality of courage, since it sprang wholly from absolute fearlessness and a Puritanical sense of duty, and was not aided by Logan's pure love of conflict, but I have never seen another man in whom this curious power over rough men was so marked.

"Go on, Youell," said Logan, more quietly than ever; and Youell went on with his prisoner—his friends following, still swearing, and with their weapons still in their hands. When the constable and the prisoner stepped into the Mayor's office, Logan stepped quickly after them and turned on the threshold, with his arm across the door. "Hold on, boys," he said, still good-naturedly; "the Mayor can attend to this.

Blue-grass and Rhododendron

If you boys want to fight anybody, fight me. I'm unarmed and you can whip me easily enough," he added, with a laugh, for he knew that passion can sometimes be turned with a jest, and that sometimes rowdies are glad to turn matters into a jest when they are getting too serious. "But you mustn't come in here," he said, as though the thing were settled beyond further discussion. For one instant—the crucial one, of course —the men hesitated, for the reason that so often makes superior numbers of no avail among the lawless—the lack of a leader of nerve—and Logan held the door without another word. But the Mayor, inside, being badly frightened, let the prisoner out at once on bond, and Logan went on the bond. Greatly disgusted, the Kentuckian went back to his office, and then and there he and his partner formed the nucleus of an organization that, so far as I know, has never had its parallel. There have been gentlemen regulators a-plenty; vigilance committees of gentlemen; the Ku-Klux Klan was originally composed of gentlemen; but I have never heard of another police-guard of gentlemen who did the every-day work of the policeman, and hewed with precision to the line of town ordinance and common law. The organization was military in character. The men began drilling and target-shooting at once. Of course, Logan was captain; his partner, Macfarlan,

Civilizing the Cumberland

was first lieutenant; a Virginian who had lost an arm in Pickett's charge at Gettysburg was second lieutenant, and a brother of mine was third.

From the beginning, times were lively, and the wise captain straightway laid down two inflexible rules for the guards. One was never to draw a pistol at all, unless necessary; never pretend to draw one as a threat or to intimidate, and never to draw unless one meant to shoot, if need be; the other was always to go in force to make an arrest. This was not only proper discretion as far as the safety of the guard was concerned, though that consideration was little thought of at the time, but it showed a knowledge of mountain-character and was extraordinarily good sense. It saved the wounded pride of the mountaineer—which is morbid. It would hurt him unspeakably to have to go home and confess that one man had put him in the calaboose, but he would not mind telling at all how he was set upon and overpowered by several. It was a tribute to his prowess, too, that so many were thought necessary. Again, he would usually give in to several without resistance; whereas he would look upon the approach of one man as a personal issue and to be met as such. This precaution saved much bloodshed, and no member of the guard failed to have opportunities a-plenty to show what he could do alone.

Blue-grass and Rhododendron

The first problem was moonshine and its faithful ally—"the blind tiger." The "tiger" is a little shanty with an ever-open mouth—a hole in the door like a post-office window. You place your money on the sill, and at the ring of the coin a mysterious arm emerges from the hole, sweeps the money away, and leaves a bottle of white whiskey. Thus you see nobody's face; and thus the owner of the beast is safe, and so are you—which you might not be if you saw and told. In every little hollow about the Gap a tiger had his lair, and these were all bearded at once by a petition to the county judge for high-license saloons, which was granted. This measure drove the tigers out of business and concentrated moonshine in the heart of the town, where its devotees were under easy guard.

Then town ordinances were passed. The wild centaurs were not allowed to ride up and down the plank walks with their reins in their teeth and firing a pistol into the ground with either hand; they could punctuate the hotel-sign no more; they could not ride at a fast gallop through the streets of the town, and—Lost Spirit of American Liberty—they could not even yell! Now when the mountaineer cannot banter with a pistol-shot and a yell, he feels hardly used indeed. The limit of indignity was reached when nobody but a policeman was allowed to blow a whistle within the

Civilizing the Cumberland

limits of the town, for the very good reason that it might be mistaken for a policeman's call and cause unnecessary excitement and exertion; or it might not be known for a policeman's call when he was really in need of help. This ordinance was suggested by Macfarlan, who blew his whistle one night, and without waiting for anybody to answer it, put two drunken Swedes under arrest. The call was not answered at once, and Macfarlan had no time or opportunity to blow again—he was too busy reducing the Swedes to subjection with his fists. Assistance came just in time to prevent them from reducing him.

These ordinances arrayed the town people against the country folks, who thought the town was doing what it pleased to prevent the country from doing anything that it pleased; they stirred up the latent spirit of the county feud, and they crystallized the most stubborn antagonism with which the guard had to deal —hostility in the adjoining county of Lee.

It was curious to note that with each element of disorder there was a climax of incident that established the recognized authority of the guard.

After the shutting down of the brick-yard, its mischief was merely merged into the general deviltry of the town, which was naturally concentrated in the high-license saloons, under the leadership of one Jack

Blue-grass and Rhòdodendron

Woods, whose local power for evil and cackling laugh seemed to mean nothing else than close personal communion with Old Nick himself. It was "nuts" to Jack to have some drunken customer blow a whistle and then stand in his door and laugh at the policemen running in from all directions. One day Jack tried it himself and Logan ran down.

"Who did that?" he asked. Jack felt bold that morning. "I blowed it." Logan thought for a moment. The ordinance against blowing a whistle had not been passed, but he made up his mind that, under the circumstances, Jack's blowing was a breach of the peace, since the guard had adopted that signal. So he said, "You mustn't do that again."

Jack had doubtless been going through precisely the same mental process, and, on the nice legal point involved, he seemed to differ.

"I'll blow it when I damn please," he said.

"Blow it again and I'll arrest you," said Logan. Jack blew. He had his right shoulder against the corner of his door at the time, and, when he raised the whistle to his lips, Logan drew and covered him before he could make another move. Woods backed slowly into his saloon to get behind his counter. Logan saw his purpose, and he closed in, taking great risk, as he always did, to avoid bloodshed, and there was a struggle. Jack managed to get his pistol out, but Logan caught him by the wrist and held the weapon away so that it was harmless as far as he was concerned; but a crowd was gathering at the door toward which the saloon-keeper's pistol was pointed, and he feared that somebody out there might be shot; so he called out:

"Drop that pistol!"

The order was not obeyed, and Logan raised his right hand high above Jack's head and dropped the butt of his weapon on Jack's skull—hard. Jack's head dropped back between his shoulders, his eyes closed, and his pistol clicked on the floor. A blow is a pretty serious thing in that part of the world, and it created great excitement. Logan himself was uneasy at Jack's trial, for fear that the saloon-keeper's friends would take the matter up; but they didn't, and, to the surprise of everybody, Jack quietly paid his fine, and, thereafter, the guard had little active trouble with Jack, though he remained always one of its bitterest enemies. This incident made the guard master of the Gap, and another extended its reputation outside.

The Howard-Turner feud was mildly active at that time over in the Kentucky Mountains not far away, and in the county of Harlan. One morning, a Howard who had killed a Turner fled from the mountains and reached the Gap, where he was wrongly suspected, arrested as a horse-thief, and put in the calaboose. A band of Turners followed him and demanded that he should be given up to them. Knowing that the man would be killed, Logan refused, and deputed a brother of mine—the third lieutenant—to take the Howard for safekeeping to the county jail, twenty miles distant. As the Turners were armed only with pistols, the third lieutenant armed his men with shot-guns, heavily loaded with buckshot, for he knew that mountaineers have no love for shot-guns. When the guards approached the calaboose, the Turners were waiting with their big pistols drawn and ready to start the fight when the Howard should be taken out. But when George Turner, the leader—a tall, good-looking, and rather chivalrous young fellow, whose death soon afterward ended the feud for a while—saw the shot-guns, he called a halt.

"Men," he said, quietly, but so that any could hear who wished, "you know that I never back down, and if you say so we'll have him or die, but we are not in our own State now; they've got the law and the shot-guns on us, and we'd better go slow." The rest readily agreed to go slow; so they put up their pistols and watched the Howard and his guards ride away. Next day some of the guard and two or three Turners inter-

Civilizing the Cumberland

changed courtesies at pool-table and bar. It was the first time, perhaps, up to that time, that the law had ever proved a serious obstacle to either faction in the gratification of personal revenge, and it seemed to make an impression, judging from the threats of vengeance that the third lieutenant got later from Harlan, and the fact that there was no more trouble from the " wild jayhawkers of old Kanetuck."

But the chief trouble was with bad men far down the valley. It looked to these as though the guard was making up trifling excuses to get them in the calaboose, and when they discovered that they would always be arrested and fined if caught riding across the side boardwalks, or blowing whistles, or shooting off their pistols, or racing their horses through the streets, they got to waiting until they were mounted and ready to go home before they started their mischief. Then they would ride at full tilt, doing everything they could that was forbidden. Logan broke up this cunning game by keeping horses saddled and ready for pursuit, and there were many and exciting chases down the valley. After several prominent mischief-makers were jailed, to their great mortification (for your bad man usually weeps copiously when he is captured—from rage as well as shame), this, too, was stopped. But great bitterness was the result, and some individual hostility was developed that resulted in several so-called "marked men"; that is, certain prominent members of the guard were picked out by the bad men for especial attention if a general fight should come up, and I believe that with several of these marked men, human nature so far got the better of an abstract motive for order and law that the compliment was heartily returned. Some of the best and some of the worst were those to be in most danger. Even a day was fixed for the evening up of old scores—a political gathering on the day that Senator Mahone was the speaker, and on that day the clash came, the story of which cannot be told here. After this clash came the boom swiftly, and the guard increased in numbers and prestige. It not only unified the best element of the town, but it had a strong influence for good on the members themselves who were young and hot-blooded. Naturally a member of the guard was morally bound not to do anything for which he would arrest another man. If a guard was unwisely indulgent he was taken to his room and kept there—a privilege that was allowed the friends of any drunken man, if he was taken out of town before he got into mischief. Many fights, and even several duels, were avoided by the new sense of personal consistency developed by the duties of the guard. Once, for instance, when the boom was at its height,

Civilizing the Cumberland

Logan determined to break up the gambling-houses of the town. Many of the guard were inveterate poker-players; so Logan merely took around an agreement to cease poker—signed by himself, and pointing out the inconsistency otherwise involved in the proposed raid. Every man signed it, stopped playing, and gambling for the time was broken up in town. By and by, some of the men down the valley began to see that the guard had no personal hostility to gratify, and that, if they came to town and behaved themselves, they would never be bothered. And they saw that the guard was as quick to arrest one of its own men as an outsider, and that it was strictly impartial in the discharge of its duties. This became evident when the jolliest and most popular man in town was put in the calaboose by his friends (he has never touched a drop of liquor since); when a guard drew his Winchester on his blood cousin and made him behave; and when another put his own brother under arrest. So local hostility died down slowly, and the guard even became popular. Membership was eagerly sought and often denied, and the force numbered a hundred men.

At last, it began to extend its operations and make expeditions out into the mountains to break up gangs of desperadoes. Once it fortified itself in the county court-house, cut port-holes through the walls, put the

Blue-grass and Rhododendron

town under martial law, and guarded the jail night and day to prevent a Kentucky mountain-clan from rescuing a murderer who had been convicted and sentenced to death; and they stayed there a month till the law was executed, and the first man ever hung in the region met death on the gallows.

After this, its work was about done, but incidents like the following continued for a year or two to be common:

One night, I saw, or rather heard, one of the guard, who is now the youngest of the nine Board of Visitors of the University of Virginia, go over a cliff thirty feet high and down into Roaring Fork with the leader of the brick-yard gang locked in his arms. The water was rather shallow, and luckily the policeman fell on top. Three of the tough's ribs were broken, and we had to carry him to the calaboose, whence he escaped, with the aid of his sweetheart, who handed him in a saw and a file; so that we had another chase after him, later, and again he ran into the river, and again, by the aid of his sweetheart, he made his final escape.

While the church-bells were ringing one morning, a drunken fellow came into town, picked up a stone from the street, and deliberately beat out a pane of glass in the door of the hardware-store so that he would not cut himself when he crawled in. Macfarlan ran

Civilizing the Cumberland

up in answer to the cry of a small boy, looked in, and, being without any weapon, got a poker from the club, next door. The tough had two butcher-knives out on the show-case, one revolver lying near them, and he was trying to load still another. He threw a butcher-knife at Macfarlan as the latter crawled in through the broken pane. Then, either he could not use his pistol at all, or he was dazed by the exhibition of such nerve, for Macfarlan, who was a lacrosse-player at Yale, and whose movements are lightning-like, downed him with the poker, and he and his brother, who was only a moment behind through the hole in the door, carried him out, unconscious.

A whistle blew one night, when a storm was going on. It came from a swamp that used to run through a part of the town. Before I could get fifty yards toward it, there were three flashes of lightning and two pistol-shots, followed by screams of terror and pain; and in a few minutes I came upon a tough writhing at the foot of a tree, and Logan bending over him. By the first flash, the captain had seen the fellow behind a tree, and he called to him to come out; by the second, he saw him levelling his pistol; and by the third flash, both fired. Logan thought at first that the man was mortally wounded, but he got well. One bitter cold night a negro shot a white man and escaped. The en-

Blue-grass and Rhododendron

tire guard watched pass and gap and railroad track for him all the awful night long. The fifteen-year-old infant of the guard—since known at Harvard as "the Colonel"—was on guard at one point alone, with orders to hold every negro who came along. When relieved, the doughty little Colonel had about twenty shivering blacks huddled and held together at the point of his pistol. Among them was the negro wanted, and that night the guard took him to the woods and spent another bitter night, guarding him from a mob.

Twice again it saved a negro from certain death. Once the crime charged was that for which the law can fix no penalty, since there is none; in Virginia it is death—death by law, as well. Some of the guard believed him guilty, and with some there was doubt; but, irrespective of belief, they answered Logan's call to guard the jail. The mob gathered, led by personal friends of the men who were on guard. As they advanced, Logan drew his pistol; he would kill the first man who advanced beyond a certain point, he said, and they knew that he meant it. After a short parley, the mob agreed not to make any attempt to take the negro out that night—their plan being to wait until he was taken to the county jail next day—and they told Logan.

"Will you give me your word that you won't?" he

The Infant of the Guard.

Civilizing the Cumberland

asked. They did, and he put up his pistol, and left the jail without a guard—it needed none. Now the curious part of this story is that several of the men who were there and ready to shoot their own friends and give up their own lives to protect the negro, had already agreed—believing in his guilt—to help take him out of the county jail, if the leaders would wait until he was without the special jurisdiction of the guard, and where the hanging would not reflect on the reputation of the Gap. Indefensible sophistry if you will, but a tribute to the influence of the captain of the guard, to the passionate *esprit du corps* that prevailed, and to the inviolability of a particular oath.

But all that is over—for the work is done. Outsiders gave the plan, the organization, the leadership, the example—the natives have done the rest. A similar awakening is all that is necessary in other mountain-communities of the South.

And such was the guard. As I was not a member until its authority was established and the danger was considerably reduced, I can pay my tribute freely. Very quickly I was led to believe that nothing was more common than courage; nothing so exceptionable as cowardice; and with that guard, nothing was. I can recall no instance in which every man was not an eager volunteer when any risk was to be run; or was not eager to shirk when the duty was to keep him out of the trouble at hand, except once. One man was willing, one night, when an attack was to be made at daybreak on a cabin full of outlaws, to stay behind and hold the horses; and this man was newly married, and was, besides, quite ill. The organization still exists to-day, and the moral effect of its existence is so strong that on the last Fourth of July, when there were several thousand people in town, not a single arrest was made. There was no need for an arrest. Four years ago the floor of the calaboose would have been many deep. And the weak old calaboose stands now, as it stood in the beginning, but, now, strong enough.

The Hanging of Talton Hall

I

THROUGH mountain and valley, humanity had talked of nothing else for weeks, and before dawn of the fatal day, humanity started in converging lines from all other counties for the county-seat of Wise—from Scott and from Lee; from wild Dickinson and Buchanan, where one may find white men who have never looked upon a black man's face; from the "Pound," which harbors the desperadoes of two sister States whose skirts are there stitched together with pine and pin-oak along the crest of the Cumberland; and, farther on, even from the far away Kentucky hills, mountain-humanity had started at dawn of the day before. A stranger would have thought that a county-fair, a camp-meeting, or a circus was the goal. Men and women, boys and girls, children and babes in arms; each in his Sunday best—the men in jeans, slouch hats, and high boots; the women in gay ribbons and brilliant homespun; in wagons and

Blue-grass and Rhododendron

on foot, on horses and mules, carrying man and man, man and boy, lover and sweetheart, or husband and wife and child—all moved through the crisp September air, past woods of russet and crimson and along brown dirt roads to a little straggling mountain-town where midway of the one long street and shut in by a tall board-fence was a court-house, with the front door closed and barred, and port-holes cut through its brick walls and looking to the rear; and in the rear a jail; and to one side of the jail, a tall wooden box with a projecting cross-beam in plain sight, from the centre of which a rope swung to and fro, when the wind moved.

Never had a criminal met death at the hands of the law in that region, and it was not sure that the law was going to take its course now; for the condemned man was a Kentucky feudsman, and his clan was there to rescue him from the gallows, and some of his enemies were on hand to see that he died a just death by a bullet, if he should manage to escape the noose. And the guard, whose grim dream of law and order seemed to be coming true, was there from the Gap, twenty miles away, to see that the noose did its ordained work. On the outskirts of the town, and along every road, boyish policemen were halting and disarming every man who carried a weapon in sight. At the back win-

The Hanging of Talton Hall

dows of the court-house and at the threatening little port-holes were more youngsters, manning Winchesters and needle-guns; at the windows of the jailer's house, which was of frame and which joined and fronted the jail, were more still on guard, and around the jail was a line of them, heavily armed to keep the crowd back on the outer side of the jail-yard fence.

The crowd had been waiting for hours. The neighboring hills were black with people, waiting; the house-tops were black with men and boys, waiting; the trees in the streets were bending under the weight of human bodies, and the jail-yard fence was full three deep with people hanging to the fence and hanging to one another's necks, waiting. Now the fatal noon was hardly an hour away, and a big man with a red face appeared at one of the jailer's windows; and then the sheriff, who began to take out the sash. At once a hush came over the crowd and then a rustling and a murmur. It was the prisoner's lawyer, and something was going to happen. Faces and gun-muzzles thickened at the port-holes and the court-house windows; the line of guards in the jail-yard wheeled and stood with their faces upturned to the window; the crowd on the fence scuffled for better positions, and the people in the locust-trees craned their necks from the branches, or climbed higher, and there was a great scraping on

Blue-grass and Rhododendron

all the roofs; even the black crowd out on the hills seemed to catch the excitement and to sway, while spots of intense blue and vivid crimson came out here and there from the blackness when the women rose from their seats on the ground. Then—sharply—there was silence. The big man disappeared, and in his place and shut in by the sashless window, as by a picture-frame, and blinking in the strong light, stood a man with black hair, cropped close, beard gone, face pale and worn, and hands that looked thin—stood Talton Hall.

He was going to confess—that was the rumor. His lawyers wanted him to confess; the preacher who had been singing hymns with him all morning wanted him to confess; the man himself wanted to confess; and now he was going to confess. What deadly mysteries he might clear up if he would! No wonder the crowd was still eager, for there was hardly a soul but knew his record—and what a record! His best friends put the list of his victims no lower than thirteen—his enemies no lower than thirty. And there, looking up at him, were three women whom he had widowed or orphaned, and at one corner of the jail-yard still another, a little woman in black—the widow of the constable whom Hall had shot to death only a year before.

Now Hall's lips opened and closed; and opened and

The Hanging of Talton Hall

closed again. Then he took hold of the side of the window and looked behind him. The sheriff brought him a chair and he sat down. Apparently he was weak and he was going to wait awhile; and so he sat, in full view, still blinking in the strong light, but nodding with a faint smile to some friend whom he could make out on the fence, or in a tree, or on a house-top, and waiting for strength to lay bare his wretched soul to man as he claimed to have laid it bare to God.

II

ONE year before, at Norton, six miles away, when the constable turned on his heel, Hall, without warning, and with the malice of Satan, shot him, and he fell on the railroad track—dead. Norton is on the Virginia side of Black Mountain, and at once Hall struck off into the woods and climbed the rocky breast of the Cumberland, to make for his native Kentucky hills.

"Somehow," he said to me, when he was in jail a year after, "I knowed right then that my name was Dennis"—a phrase of evil prophecy that he had picked up outside the mountains. He swore to me that, the night of the murder, when he lay down to sleep, high on the mountain-side and under some rhododendron-bushes, a flock of little birds flew in on him like a gust of rain and perched over and around him, twittering at him all night long. At daybreak they were gone, but now and then throughout the day, as he sat in the sun planning his escape, the birds would sweep chattering over his head, he said, and would sweep chattering back again. He swore to me further, on the day he was to go to the scaffold (I happened to be on the death-watch that morning), that at daybreak those birds had come again to his prison-window and had chirped at him through the bars. All this struck me as strange, for Hall's brain was, on all other points, as clear as rain, and, unlike "The Red Fox of the Mountains," who occupied the other cell of his cage, was not mystical, and never claimed to have visions. Hall was a Kentucky feudsman—one of the mountain-border ruffians who do their deeds of deviltry on one side of the State-line that runs the crest of Black Mountain, and then step over to the other side to escape the lax arm of mountain-justice. He was little sorry for what he had done, except, doubtless, for the reason that the deed would hamper his freedom. He must move elsewhere, when a pair of hot black eyes were at that moment luring him back to Norton. Still, he could have the woman follow him, and his temporary denial bothered him but little. In reality,

The Hanging of Talton Hall

he had not been much afraid of arrest and trial, in spite of the birds and his premonition. He had come clear of the charge of murder many times before, but he claimed afterward that he was more uneasy than he had ever been; and with what good reason he little knew. Only a few miles below where he sat, and beyond the yawning mouth that spat the little branch trickling past his feet as a torrent through the Gap and into Powell's Valley, was come a new power to take his fate in hand. Down there—the Gap itself was a hell-hole then—a little band of "furriners" had come in from blue-grass Kentucky and tide-water Virginia to make their homes; young fellows in whom pioneering was a birthright; who had taken matters into their own hands, had formed a volunteer police-guard, and were ready, if need be, to match Winchester with Winchester, pistol with pistol, but always for and in the name of the law. Talt had one enemy, too, to whom he gave little thought. This was old "Doc" Taylor—a queer old fellow, who was preacher, mountain-doctor, revenue-officer; who preached Swedenborgianism—Heaven knows where he got it in those wilds—doctored with herbs night and day for charity, and chased criminals from vanity, or personal enmity, or for fun. He knew every by-path through the mountains, and he moved so swiftly that the superstitious credited him with superhuman powers of locomotion. Nobody was surprised, walking some lonely path, to have old Doc step from the bushes at his side and as mysteriously slip away. He had a spy-glass fully five feet long with which to watch his quarry from the mountain-tops, and he wore moccasins with the heels forward so that nobody could tell which way he had gone. In time his cunning gave him the title of "The Red Fox of the Mountains." It was the Red Fox who hated Hall and was to catch him; the "furriners from the Gap" were to guard him, see that he was tried by a fearless jury, and, if pronounced guilty, hanged. Hall knew Taylor's hatred, of course, but scorned him, and he had heard vaguely of the Gap. In prison, he alternately cursed his cell-mate, who, by a curious turn of fate, was none other than the Red Fox caught, at last, in his own toils, and wondered deeply, and with hearty oaths, "what in the hell" people at the Gap had against him that they should leave their business and risk their lives to see that he did not escape a death that was unmerited. The mountaineer finds abstract devotion to law and order a hard thing to understand. The Red Fox more than hated Hall—he feared him; and how Hall, after capture, hated him! No sooner was the feudsman's face turned southward than the Red

The Hanging of Talton Hall

Fox kept cunning guard over the black-eyed woman at Norton and, through her, learned where his enemy was. More—he furnished money for two detectives to go after Hall and arrest him on a charge of which he was not guilty, and thus decoy him, without resistance, to jail, where they told him the real reason of the arrest. Hall fell to the floor in a cursing fit of rage. Then the Red Fox himself went south to help guard Hall back to the mountains. A mob of the dead constable's friends were waiting for him at Norton—for the murder was vicious and unprovoked—and old Doc stood by Hall's side, facing the infuriated crowd with a huge drawn pistol in each hand and a peculiar smile on his washed-out face. Old Squire Salyers, father-in-law to the constable, made a vicious cut at the prisoner with a clasp knife as he stepped from the train, but he was caught and held, and with the help of the volunteer guard from the Gap, Hall was got safely to jail at Gladeville, the county-seat of Wise.

It was to protect Hall from his enemies that concerned Hall's Kentucky mountain-clan at first, for while trial for murder was not rare and conviction was quite possible, such a thing as a hanging had never been heard of in that part of the world. Why, then, the Red Fox was so eager to protect Hall for the law was a mystery to many, but the truth probably was that he had mischief of his own to conceal; and, moreover, he knew about that guard at the Gap. So, during the trial, the old man headed the local guard that led Hall to and from jail to court-house, and stood by him in the court-room with one of the big pistols ever drawn and that uncanny smile on his uncanny face. For the Red Fox had a strange face. One side was calm, kindly, benevolent; on the other side a curious twitch of the muscles would now and then lift the corner of his mouth into a wolfish snarl. So that Dr. Jekyll and Mr. Hyde in old Doc were separated only by the high bridge of his nose. Throughout the long trial, old Doc was at his post. Only one night was he gone, and the next morning an old moonshiner and four of his family were shot from ambush in the "Pound." As Doc was back at his post that afternoon, nobody thought of connecting the murder with him. Besides, everybody was concerned with the safety of Hall—his enemies and his friends: his friends for one reason, that eight of the jury were fearless citizens of the "Gap" who would give a verdict in accordance with the law and the evidence, in spite of the intimidation that, hitherto, had never failed to bring a desperado clear; and for another, that the coils were surely tightening; his enemies, for

The Hanging of Talton Hall

fear that Hall's friends would cheat the gallows by rescuing him from jail. Rumors of rescue thickened every day—Hall's Kentucky clan was coming over Black Mountain to take the prisoner from jail. Moreover, Hall's best friend—John Rawn—was the most influential man in the county—a shrewd, daring fellow who kept a band of armed retainers within call of his yard-fence. He, too, it was said, was going to help Hall to freedom. Accordingly the day before the verdict was brought in, twenty of the volunteer guard came up from the Gap, twenty miles away, to keep Hall's friends from saving him from the gallows, and his enemies from rescuing him for death by a Winchester; and to do this they gave it out that they would put him aboard at Norton; but, instead, they spirited him away across the hills to another railroad.

A few months later Hall was brought back for execution. He was placed in a cage that had two cells, and, as he passed the first cell an old freckled hand was thrust between the bars to greet him and a voice called him by name. Hall stopped in amazement; then he burst out laughing; then he struck at the pallid face through the bars with his manacles and cursed him bitterly; then he laughed again, horribly. It was the Red Fox behind the bars on charge of shooting the moonshiner's family from ambush—the Red

Blue-grass and Rhododendron

Fox caught in his own toils; and there the two stayed in adjoining cells of the same cage. The Red Fox sang hymns by day, and had visions by night, which he told to the death-watch every morning. In one dream that he told me he said he was crossing a river in a boat. The wind rose, a storm came, and he barely got to land. Wind and wave were his enemies, he said; the storm was his trial, and getting to shore meant that he was coming out all right.

The Red Fox's terror of Hall was pathetic. Once he wrote to my brother, who was first in command in the absence of the captain of the guard: "This man iS a Devil and i am a fraid of him he is trying to burn the gail down and i wiSh you would take him away." But the two stayed together—the one waiting for trial, the other for his scaffold, which was building. The sound of saw and hammer could be plainly heard throughout the jail, but Hall said never a word about it.

He thought he was going to be pardoned, and if not pardoned—rescued, surely. He did get a stay of execution for a month, and then the rumors of rescue flew about in earnest, and the guard came up from the Gap in full force and cut port-holes in the court-house walls, and drilled twice a day and put out sentinels at night. The town was practically under military law, and the

The Hanging of Talton Hall

times were tender. By day we would see suspicious characters watching us from the spurs round about, and hear very queer noises at night. The senses of the young guards got so acute because of the strain, that one swore that he heard a cat walking over the sand a hundred yards away. Another was backed into town one dark night by an old cow that refused to halt, when challenged. Another picket let off his gun by accident just before day, and the men sprang from their blankets on the court-house floor and were at the windows and port-holes like lightning. Two who waited to dress, were discharged next morning. One night there was a lively discussion when the captain gave strict orders that the pickets must fire as soon as they saw the mob, in order to alarm the guard in town, and not wait until they were personally safe. This meant the sacrifice of that particular picket, and there was serious question as to the right of the captain to give orders like that. And that night as I passed through the room where the infant of the guard was waiting to go on picket duty on a lonely road at midnight, I heard him threshing around in his bed, and he called to me in the manner of a farewell:

"I—I—I've made up my mind to shoot," he said; and so had everybody else. Whether a thing happens or not makes little difference as far as the interest of

Blue-grass and Rhododendron

it is concerned, when one is convinced that it is going to happen and looking for it to take place any minute; at least, waiting out on a lonely road under the stars, alone, for a band of " wild jayhawkers from old Kanetuck " to come sweeping down on the town was quite enough to keep the pickets awake and alert. One night we thought trouble was sure, and, indeed, serious trouble almost came, but not the trouble we were expecting. A lawyer brought the news that two bands of Kentuckians had crossed Black Mountain that morning to fire the town at both ends and dynamite the court-house and the jail. As there were only fifteen of us on hand, we telegraphed speedily to the Gap for the rest of the guard, and an engine and a caboose were sent down for them from Norton, six miles away. The engineer was angry at having extra work to do, and when he started from the Gap with the guard, he pulled his throttle wide open. The road was new and rough, and the caboose ran off the track while going through a tunnel; ran along the ties for several hundred yards and ran across sixty feet of trestle, striking a girder of the bridge and splitting it for two yards or more. A guard managed to struggle out of the door and fire off his Winchester just there, and the engineer, hearing it, pulled up within ten yards of a sharp curve. The delay of ten seconds in the report

The Hanging of Talton Hall

of the gun, and the caboose, with the thirty-five occupants, would have been hurled down an embankment and into the river. The Kentuckians did not come in that night, and thereafter the guard stayed at the county-seat in full force until the day set for the execution.

Apparently the purpose of a rescue was given up, but we could not tell, and one morning there was considerable excitement when John Rawn, the strong friend of the condemned man, rode into town and up to the jail, and boldly asked permission to see Hall. Rawn was the man to whom Hall was looking for rescue. He was a tall, straight fellow with blond hair and keen blue eyes. The two had been comrades in the war, and Hall had been Rawn's faithful ally in his many private troubles. Two of us were detailed to be on hand at the meeting, and I was one of the two. Hall came to the cell-door, and the men grasped hands and looked at each other for a full minute without saying a word. The eyes of both filled.

"Of course, Talt," he said, finally, "I want the law to take its course. I don't want to do anything against the law and I know you don't want me to." I looked for a sly quiver of an eyelid after this speech, but Rawn seemed sincere, and Hall, I thought, dropped, as though some prop had suddenly been knocked from under him. He looked down quickly, but he mumbled:

"Yes, of course, that's right, I reckon. We don't want to do nothing agin the law."

Still, he never believed he was going to hang, nor did he give up hope even on the morning of his execution when the last refusal to interfere came in from the Governor—the chance of rescue still was left. The preachers had been coming in to sing and pray with him, and a priest finally arrived; for, strange to say, Hall was a Catholic—the only one I ever saw in the mountains. Occasionally, too, there had come his sister, a tall, spare woman dressed in black; and she could hardly look at a member of the guard except with the bitterest open hatred. All these besought Hall to repent, and, in time, he did; but his sincerity was doubtful. Once, for instance, in a lull between the hymns, and after Hall had forgiven his enemies, the infant, who was on the death-watch, passed near the prisoner's cell-door, and Hall's hand shot through the bars and the tips of his fingers brushed the butt of the boy's pistol, which protruded from a holster on his hip.

"Not this time, Talt," he said, springing away.

"I was only foolin'," Talt said, but his eyes gleamed.

The Hanging of Talton Hall

Again, the night before, being on guard down behind the jail, I heard Hall cursing because the guards would give him no whiskey. This was cruel, for the reason that they had been allowing him liquor until that night, when he was most in need of it. As soon as I was relieved, I got a bottle of whiskey and told the watch to let him have it. Hall was grateful, and next morning he called me by my first name.

"I love you," he said, "but I've got you spotted."

He had repeatedly sworn that he would have many of us ambushed, after his death, and his sister was supposed to have our names and descriptions of us, and an old Kentucky mountaineer told me that he would rather have the ten worst men in the mountains his deadly enemies than that one woman. Hall meant that he had me on his list. As ambush would be very easy on our trips to and from the county-seat, through thick laurel and rhododendron, I told the priest of Hall's threat and suggested that he might save us trouble by getting Hall to announce in his confession that he wanted nothing else done. The priest said he would try. But for a little while on the morning of the execution, Hall, for the first time, gave up and got very humble; and there was one pathetic incident. The sister was crouched at the cell-door, and Hall, too, was crouched on the floor, talking to her through the bars. They spoke in a low tone, but were not permitted to whisper. At last Hall asked that he might give his sister a secret message. It had nothing to do with the guard, or the law, or his escape, but he did not want it heard. The "Judge," who was on guard, was tenderhearted, but a martinet withal, and he felt obliged to deny the request. And then Hall haltingly asked aloud that his sister should bring a silk handkerchief and tie it around his throat—afterward—to hide the red mark of the rope. Tears sprang to the "Judge's" eyes, and he coughed quickly and pulled out his own handkerchief to blow his nose. It happened to be of silk, and, a moment later, I saw him pressing the handkerchief into the woman's hands. An hour later Hall said that he was ready to confess.

III

No wonder the crowd was eager. Would he tell all? How, when he was only fourteen years old, he had shot Harry Maggard, his uncle, during the war—Hall denied this; how he had killed his two brothers-in-law —one was alive, Hall said, and he had been tried for killing the other and had come clear; how he had killed Henry Monk in the presence of Monk's wife at a wild-

The Hanging of Talton Hall

bee tree—he claimed to have been cleared for that; how he had killed a Kentucky sheriff by dropping to the ground when the sheriff fired, in this way dodging the bullet and then shooting the officer from where he lay, supposedly dead—that, Hall said, was a lie; how he had taken Mack Hall's life in the Wright-Jones feud—Mack, he said, had waylaid and wounded him first; how he had thrown John Adams out of the courthouse window at Prestonburg, over in Kentucky, and broken his neck—Adams was drunk, Hall said, and fell out; why he had killed Abe Little—because, said Hall, he resisted arrest; how and where he killed Red-necked Johnson, who was found out in the woods one morning a week after he had disappeared; whether he had killed Frank Salyers, whose wife he afterward married; and the many other mysteries that he might clear up if he would speak. Would he tell all? No wonder the crowd was still.

Hall stood motionless, and his eyes slowly wandered around at the waiting people—in the trees, on the roofs, and on the fence—and he sank slowly back to his chair again. Again a murmur rose. Maybe he was too weak to stand and talk—perhaps he was going to talk from his chair; yes, he was leaning forward now and his lips were opening. He was looking downward into the uplooking face of a big, red-cheeked fellow, and he was surely going to speak. The crowd became still again. And he did speak.

"What's yo' name?" he asked. The fellow told him—he had been an unimportant witness in the trial—neither for nor against Hall.

"I thought so," said Hall, and of his own accord he turned away from the window and that was all that the man with the charge of two-score murders on his soul had to say to the world before he left it to be judged for them, as he firmly believed, by a living God. A little later the line of guards wheeled again to face the crowded fence, and Hall started for the scaffold. He kissed my brother's hand in the jail, and when old Doc came to his cell-door to tell him good-by, Hall put his face to the window and kissed his bitterest enemy—the man who had brought him to his death. Then he went out with a firm step; but his face was dispirited and hopeless at last; it looked the face of a man who has just been relieved from some long-endured physical pain that has left him weak in body and spirit. Twenty of us had been assigned by lot to duty as a special guard inside the box, and all of us, at his request, shook one of his helpless hands, which were tied behind his back. 'When he had mounted the scaffold, he called for his sister, and the tall, thin, black spectre came in and mounted the scaffold, too, stopping

Hall stood as motionless as the trunk of an oak.

The Hanging of Talton Hall

on the step below him. Hall did not call her by name —he hardly looked at her, nor did he tell her good-by again.

"Been enough killin' on my account," he said, abruptly; " I don't want nothin' more done about this. I don't want no more lives lost on account o' me. I want things to stop right here."

The woman waved a threatening hand over us, and her voice rose in a wail. " Oh, Talt, I can't let this rest here. You'd just as well take up one o' these men right here and hang 'em. I ain't goin' to let it stop here—no—no!" And she began to cry and ran down the steps and out of the box.

Hall stood as motionless as the trunk of an oak. A man will show nervousness with a twitch of the lips, a roll of the eyes, or, if in no other way, with his hands; but I was just behind him, and not a finger of his bound hands moved. The sheriff was a very tenderhearted man and a very nervous one; and the arrangements for the execution were awkward. Two upright beams had to be knocked from under the trap-door, so that it would rest on the short rope-noose that had to be cut before the door would fall. As each of these was knocked out, the door sank an inch, and the suspense was horrible. The poor wretch must have thought that each stroke was the one that was to send him to eternity, but not a muscle moved. All was ready, at last, and the sheriff cried, in a loud voice:

"May God have mercy on this poor man's soul!" and struck the rope with a common hatchet. The black-capped apparition shot down, and the sheriff ran, weeping, out of the door of the box.

So far no revenge has been taken for the hanging of Talton Hall. The mountaineer never forgets, and he hates as long as he remembers, but it is probable that no trouble will ever come of it unless some prominent member of that guard should chance, some day, to wander carelessly into the little creek to which the rough two-horse wagon followed by relatives and friends, mounted and on foot, bore the remains of the first victim of law and order in the extreme southwest corner of the commonwealth of Virginia.

The Red Fox of the Mountains

THE Red Fox of the Mountains was going to be hanged. Being a preacher, as well as herb-doctor, revenue-officer, detective, crank, and assassin, he was going to preach his own funeral sermon on the Sunday before the day set for his passing. He was going to wear a suit of white and a death-cap of white, both made of damask tablecloth by his little old wife, and both emblems of the purple and fine linen that he was to put on above. Moreover, he would have his body kept unburied for three days—saying that, on the third day, he would arise and go about preaching. How he reconciled such a dual life at one and the same time, over and under the stars, was known only to his twisted brain, and is no concern of mine—I state the facts. But had such a life been possible, it would have been quite consistent with the Red Fox's strange dual way on earth. For, on Sundays he preached the Word; other days, he was a walking arsenal, with a huge 50 x 75 Winchester over one

Blue-grass and Rhododendron

shoulder, two belts of gleaming cartridges about his waist, and a great pistol swung to either hip. In the woods, he would wear moccasins with the heels forward, so that no man could tell which way he had gone. You might be walking along a lonely path in the mountains and the Red Fox—or " old Doc "—as he was usually called, would step mysteriously from the bushes at your side, ask a few questions and, a few hundred yards farther, would disappear again—to be heard of again—a few hours later—at some incredible distance away. Credited thus with superhuman powers of locomotion and wearing those mysterious moccasins—and, as a tribute to his infernal shrewdness—he came to be known, by and by, as " The Red Fox of the Mountains." Sometimes he would even carry a huge spy-glass, five feet long, with which he watched his enemies from the mountain-tops. When he had " located " them, he would slip down and take a pot shot at them. And yet, day or night, he would, as " yarb-doctor," walk a dozen miles to see a sick friend, and charge not a cent for his services. And day and night he would dream dreams and have visions and talk his faith by the hour. One other dark deed had been laid to his door—unproven—but now, caught in his own toils, at last, the Red Fox was going to be hanged.

The Red Fox of the Mountains

The scene of that death-sentence was a strange one. The town was a little mountain-village—a county-seat—down in the southwestern corner of Virginia, and not far from the Kentucky line. The court-house was of brick, but rudely built.

The court-room was crowded and still, and the Judge shifted uneasily in his chair—for it was his first death-sentence—and leaned forward on his elbows—speaking slowly:

"Have you anything to say whereby sentence of death should not be pronounced on you?"

The Red Fox rose calmly, shifted his white tie, cleared his throat, and stood a moment, steady and silent, with his strange dual character showing in his face—kindness and benevolence on one side, a wolfish snarl on the other, and both plain to any eye that looked.

"No," he said, clearly, "but I have one friend here who I would like to speak for me."

Again the Judge shifted in his chair. He looked at the little old woman who sat near, in black—wife to the Red Fox and mother of his children.

"Why," he said, "why—yes—but who is your friend?"

"Jesus Christ!" said the Red Fox, sharply. The whole house shivered, and the Judge reverently bowed his head.

Blue-grass and Rhododendron

Only a few months before, I had seen the Red Fox in that same court-room. But, then, he had a huge pistol in each hand and bore himself like a conqueror, as he guarded his old enemy, Talton Hall, to and fro from court-house to jail, and stood over him in the court-room while that old enemy was on trial for his life. To be sure, that flying wedge of civilization—the volunteer police-guard down at the "Gap," twenty miles away, was on hand, too, barricading the court-house, through the brick walls of which they had cut port-holes, keeping the town under military law, and on guard, night and day, to prevent Hall's Kentucky clansmen from rescuing him; but it was the Red Fox who furnished money and brains to run his enemy down—who guarded him to jail and who stood at the railway station, with his big pistols and his strange smile, keeping at bay the mob who hungered for Hall's life without the trial by his peers. And now, where Hall had stood then,—the Red Fox was standing now, with the cross-beam of the gallows from which Hall had dangled, and from which the Fox was to dangle now,—plain to his eyes through the open window. It was a curious transformation in so short a time from the hunter-of-men to the hunted-of-men, and it was still more curious that, just while the Red Fox was hounding Hall to his grave, he should have done the

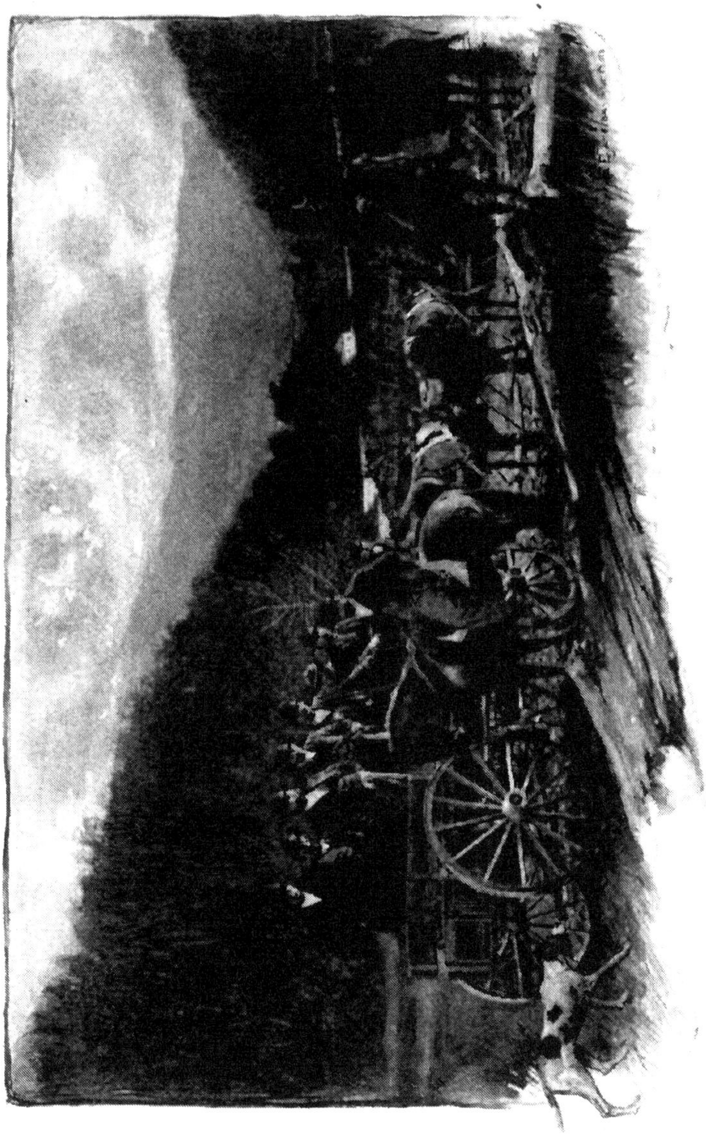

The Red Fox of the Mountains

deed that, straightway and soon, was to lead him there.

For the Red Fox had one other bitter enemy whom he feared even more than he hated—an old moonshiner from the Pound—who came to the little county-seat every court-day. Indeed, a certain two-horse wagon, driven by a thin, little, old woman and a big-eared, sallow-faced boy, used to be a queer sight on the dirty streets of the town; for the reason that the woman and boy rarely left the wagon, and both were always keenly watchful and rather fearful of something that lay on straw behind the seat. This something, you soon discovered, was the out-stretched body of a huge, gaunt, raw-boned mountaineer, so badly paralyzed that he could use nothing but his head and his deep-sunken, keen, dark eyes. The old man had a powerful face, and his eyes were fierce and wilful. He was well known to the revenue service of North Carolina, and in a fight with the officers of that State, a few years previous, he had got the wounds that had put him on his back, unable to move hand or foot.

He was carried thence to the Pound in Kentucky, where he lived and ran his "wild-cat" stills, undeterred by the law or the devil. Ira Mullins—old Ira Mullins—was his name, and once when the Red Fox was in the revenue service, the two came into con-

Blue-grass and Rhododendron

flict. Ira was bringing some " moonshine " back from North Carolina in a wagon, and the Red Fox waited for him at the county-seat with a posse, and opened fire on Mullins and two companions from behind fence and house corner. (There are some who say that the Fox fired from a very safe position indeed.) Only one was killed; the horses ran away and carried off the body and left the other two on foot. A little later, old Ira walked leisurely up the street and on out of town, unmolested and unfollowed. This was supposed to be the origin of the trouble between Mullins, moonshiners, and the Red Fox of the Mountains.

One day, while Talton Hall was on trial and the Red Fox was guarding him, old Ira came to town. Two days later the Red Fox disappeared over night, and the next morning, just while old Ira, his wife, his big-eared son of fourteen years, a farm-hand, old Ira's brother, and that brother's wife were turning a corner of the road through Pound Gap, and, just under some great rocks on a little spur above them, sheets of fire blazed in the sunlight and the roar of Winchesters rose. Only two got away: the boy, whose suspenders were cut in two, as he ran up the road, and the brother's wife, who was allowed to escape back into Virginia and who gave the alarm. Behind the rocks were found some bits of a green veil, a heap of cartridge shells, and an

The Red Fox of the Mountains

old army haversack. There were large twigs which had been thrust into crevices between the rocks about waist high. These were withered, showing that some of the assassins had been waiting for the victims for days. Who had done the murder was a mystery. The old woman, who had escaped, said there were three men, and so there turned out to be; that they had the upper part of their faces covered with green veils; and that she thought two of the men were Cal and Heenan Fleming of the Pound and that the third was the Red Fox of the Mountains. Some of the empty shells that were found behind the " blind " fitted a 50 x 75 Winchester, and only three of such guns were known in the mountains. It was learned later that the Red Fox had one of these three. The shells found were rim-fire, instead of centre-fire, as the Fox on his trial tried to prove that his shells were. An examination of the gun proved that some friend had tried to alter it; but the job was so bungling that it was plain that tinkering had been done. So that the Winchester and the effort of this unskilful friend and the old man's absence from his post of duty on the night preceding the murder, made it plain that the Red Fox had had a hand in the murder; so that when Hall—who, after his sentence, had been taken away for safe-keeping, was brought back to the county-seat for execution—

there was the Red Fox in the adjoining cell of the same cage whose door was to close on Hall. And as Hall passed, the Red Fox thrust out a freckled paw to shake hands, but Hall struck at him with his manacles and cursed him bitterly. And in those cells the two enemies waited—the one for the scaffold that both could hear building outside, and the other for the trial that was to put his feet on the same trap-door. The Red Fox swung in a hammock, reading his Bible by day and having visions at night, which he would interpret to me, when I was on Hall's death-watch, as signs of his own innocence and his final freedom among the hills. Nothing delighted Hall more, meanwhile, at that time, than to torture his old enemy.

"I know I'm purty bad," he would say—"but thar's lots wuss men than me in the world—old Doc in thar, for instance." For "old Doc" by virtue of his herb practice was his name as well as the Red Fox of the Mountains. And the old Fox would go on reading his Bible.

Then Hall would say:

"Oh, thar ain't nothin' twixt ole Doc and me— 'cept this iron wall," and he would kick the thin wall so savagely that the Red Fox would pray unavailingly to be removed to another part of the jail.

And when the day of Hall's execution came, he got

The Red Fox of the Mountains

humble and kissed the first lieutenant's hand—and he forgave the Red Fox and asked to kiss him. And the Red Fox gave him the Judas-kiss through the grating of his cell-door and, when Hall marched out, took out his watch and stood by the cell-door listening eagerly. Presently the fall of the trap-door echoed through the jail—"Th-o-o-m-p!" The Red Fox glued his eyes to the watch in his hand. The second hand went twice around its circuit and he snapped the lid and gave a deep sigh of relief:

"Well, he's gone now," said the Red Fox, and he went back in peace to his hammock and his Bible.

The Red Fox was no seer in truth, and his interpretations of his own visions proved him no prophet.

And so, finally, where Hall had stood, the Red Fox of the Mountains was standing now, and where, in answer to the last question of the Judge, Hall had sat in sullen silence, the Red Fox rose to ask that a friend might speak for him—startling the court-room:

"Jesus Christ."

Thereupon, of course, the Red Fox lifted a Bible from the desk before him and for one half hour read verses that bore on his own innocence and burned with fire and damnation for his enemies. The plea was useless. Useless was the silent, eloquent, piteous plea of the little old woman in black who sat near him. The Red Fox was doomed.

The guard down at "the Gap" had done its duty with Talton Hall, but it was the policy of the guard to let the natives uphold the law whenever they would and could; and so the guard went home to the Gap while the natives policed the jail and kept old Doc safe. To be sure, little care was necessary, for the Red Fox did not have the friends who would have flocked to the rescue of Talton Hall.

That funeral sermon was preached on the Sunday before the day, and a curious crowd gathered to hear him. The Red Fox was led from the jail; he stood on the porch of the jailer's house with a little table in front of him; on it lay a Bible; on the other side of the table sat a little, pale-faced, old woman in black, with a black sunbonnet drawn close to her face. By the side of the Bible lay a few pieces of bread. It was the Red Fox's last communion on earth—a communion which he administered to himself and in which there was no other soul on earth to join, except the little old woman in black.

It was pathetic beyond words, when the old fellow lifted the bread and asked the crowd to come forward to partake with him in the last sacrament. Not a soul moved. Only the little old woman who had been ill-treated, deserted by the old fellow for many

The Red Fox of the Mountains

years; only she of all the crowd gave any answer, and she turned her face for one instant timidly toward him. With a churlish gesture the old man pushed the bread over toward her, and with hesitating, trembling fingers she reached for it.

The sermon that followed was rambling, denunciatory, and unforgiving. Never did he admit guilt.

On the last day, the Red Fox appeared in his white suit of tablecloth. The little old woman in black had even made the cap which was to be drawn over his face at the last moment—and she had made that, too, of white. He walked firmly to the scaffold-steps and stood there for one moment blinking in the sunlight, his head just visible over the rude box, some twenty feet square, that surrounded him—a rude contrivance to shield the scene of his death. For one moment he looked at the sky and the trees with a face that was white and absolutely expressionless; then he sang one hymn of two verses. The white cap was drawn, and the strange old man was launched on the way to that world in which he believed so firmly, and toward which he had trod so strange a way on earth.

The little old woman in black, as he wished, had the body kept for three days, unburied. His ghost, the mountaineers say, walks lonely paths of the Cumberland to this day, but—the Red Fox never rose.

Man-Hunting in the Pound

THE pale lad from the Pound was telling news to an eager circle of men just outside the open window of the little mountain-hotel, and, inside, I dropped knife and fork to listen. The wily old "Daddy" of the Fleming boys had been captured; the sons were being hemmed in that very day, and a fight between sheriff's posse and outlaws was likely any hour.

Ten minutes later I was astride a gray mule, and with an absurd little .32 Smith & Wesson popgun on my hip—the only weapon I could find in town—was on my way to the Pound.

Our volunteer police-guard down at "The Gap," twenty miles away, was very anxious to capture those Fleming boys. Talton Hall, feud-leader and desperado, had already been hanged, and so had his bitter enemy, the Red Fox of the Mountains. With the Fleming outlaws brought to justice, the fight of the guard for law and order was about won. And so, as

Blue-grass and Rhododendron

I was a member of that guard, it behooved me to hurry—which I did.

The Gap is in the southwestern corner of old Virginia, and is a ragged gash down through the Cumberland Mountains to the water level of a swift stream that there runs through a mountain of limestone and between beds of iron ore and beds of coking coal. That is why some threescore young fellows gathered there from Blue-grass Kentucky and Tide-water Virginia not many years ago, to dig their fortunes out of the earth. Nearly all were college graduates, and all were high-spirited, adventurous and well-born. They proposed to build a town and, incidentally, to make cheaper and better iron there than was made anywhere else on the discovered earth.

A "boom" came. The labor and capital question was solved instantly, for every man in town was straightway a capitalist. You couldn't get a door hung—every carpenter was a meteoric Napoleon of finance. Every young blood in town rode Blue-grass saddle-horses and ate eight-o'clock dinners—making many dollars each day and having high jinks o' nights at the club, which, if you please, entertained, besides others of distinction, a duke and duchess who had wearily eluded the hospitality of New York. The

Man-Hunting in the Pound

woods were full of aristocrats and plutocrats—American and English. The world itself seemed to be moving that way, and the Gap stretched its jaws wide with a grin of welcome. Later, you could get a door hung, but here I draw the veil. It was magnificent, but it was not business.

At the high tide, even, the Gap was, however, something of a hell-hole for several reasons; and the clash of contrasts was striking. The Kentucky feudsmen would chase each other there, now and then, from over Black Mountain; and the toughs on the Virginia side would meet there on Saturdays to settle little differences of opinion and sentiment. They would quite take the town sometimes—riding through the streets, yelling and punctuating the sign of our one hotel with pistol-bullet periods to this refrain:

..... G.r.a.n.d C.e.n.t.r.a.l H.o.t.e.l .....
Hell! Hell! Hell!

—keeping time, meanwhile, like darkies in a hoedown. Or, a single horseman might gallop down one of our wooden sidewalks, with his reins between his teeth, and firing into the ground with a revolver in each hand. All that, too, was magnificent, but it was not business. The people who kept store would have to close up and take to the woods.

Blue-grass and Rhododendron

And thus arose a unique organization—a volunteer police-guard of gentlemen, who carried pistol, billy, and whistle, and did a policeman's work—hewing always strictly to the line of the law.

The result was rather extraordinary. The Gap soon became the only place south of Mason and Dixon's line, perhaps, where a street fight of five minutes' duration, or a lynching, was impossible. A yell, a pistol-shot, or the sight of a drunken man, became a rare occurrence. Local lawlessness thus subdued, the guard extended its benign influence—creating in time a public sentiment fearless enough to convict a desperado, named Talt Hall; and, guarding him from rescue by his Kentucky clansmen for one month at the county-seat, thus made possible the first hanging that mountain-region had ever known.

After that the natives, the easy-going, tolerant good people, caught the fever for law and order, for, like lawlessness, law, too, is contagious. It was they who guarded the Red Fox, Hall's enemy, to the scaffold, and it was they who had now taken up our hunt for the Red Fox's accomplices—the Fleming outlaws of the Pound.

We were anxious to get those boys—they had evaded and mocked us so long. Usually they lived in a cave, but lately they had grown quite "tame."

Man-Hunting in the Pound

From working in the fields, dressed in women's clothes, they got to staying openly at home and lounging around a cross-roads store at the Pound. They even had the impudence to vote for a sheriff and a county judge. They levied on their neighbors for food and clothes, and so bullied and terrorized the Pound that nobody dared to deny them whatever they asked, or dared to attempt an arrest. At last, they got three or four recruits, and tying red strips of flannel to their shoulders and Winchesters, drilled in the county road, mocking our drill at the county-seat when we were guarding Talton Hall.

This taunt was a little too much, and so we climbed on horseback late one afternoon, wrapped our guns in overcoats, and started out for an all-night ride, only to be turned back again at the foot of Black Mountain by our captain and first lieutenant, who had gone over ahead of us as spies. The outlaws were fighting among themselves; one man was killed, and we must wait until they got "tame" again.

A few weeks later the guard rode over again, dashed into the Fleming cabin at daybreak and captured a houseful of screaming women and children —to the great disgust of the guard and to the great humor of the mountaineers, who had heard of our coming and gone off, dancing, down the road only an hour before. It was then that the natives, emulating our example, took up the search. They were doing the work now, and it was my great luck to be the only member of the guard who knew what was going on.

The day was hot, the road dusty, and the gray mule was slow. Within two hours I was at the head of the Pound—a wild, beautiful, lawless region that harbored the desperadoes of Virginia and Kentucky, who could do mischief in either State and step to refuge across the line. Far ahead, I could see a green dip in the mountains where the Red Fox and the Fleming boys had shot the Mullins family of moonshiners to death from ambush one sunny morning in May.

Below, sparkled Pound River roaring over a mill-day, and by the roadside, as I went down, I found the old miller alone. The posse of natives had run upon the Flemings that morning, he said, and the outlaws, after a sharp fight, had escaped—wounded. The sheriff was in charge of the searching party, and he believed that the Flemings would be caught now, for sure.

"Which way?" I asked.

The old fellow pointed down a twisting, sunlit ravine, dense with woods, and I rode down the dim

Man-Hunting in the Pound

creek that twisted through it. Half an hour later I struck a double log-cabin with quilts hanging in its windows—which was unusual. An old woman appeared in the doorway—a tall, majestic old tigress, with head thrown back and a throat so big that it looked as though she had a goitre.

"Who lives here?"

"The Flemingses lives hyeh," she said, quietly.

I was startled. I had struck the outlaws' cabin by chance, and so, to see what I might learn, I swung from the gray mule and asked for a glass of buttermilk. A handsome girl of twenty, a Fleming sister, with her dress open at the throat, stepped from the door and started to the spring-house. Through the door I could see another woman—wife of one of the outlaws—ill. A "base-born" child toddled toward me, and a ten-year-old boy—a Fleming brother—with keen eyes and a sullen face, lay down near me—watching me, like a snake in the grass.

The old woman brought out a chair and lighted a pipe.

"Whar air ye from, and what mought yo' name be?"

I evaded half the inquiry.

"I come from the Blue-grass, but I'm living at the Gap just now." She looked at me keenly, as did the snake in the grass, and I turned my chair so that I could watch that boy.

"Was you over hyeh that night when them fellows from the Gap run in on us?"

"No."

The old woman's big throat shook with quiet laughter. The girl laughed and the woman through the door laughed in her apron, but the boy's face moved not a muscle. It was plain that we had no monopoly of the humor of that daybreak dash into a house full of women and children.

"One fool feller stuck his head up into the loft and lit a match to see if my boys was up thar. *Lit a match!* He wouldn't 'a' had no head ef they had been." She laughed again, and drew on her pipe.

"I give 'em coffee," she went on, "while they waited for my boys to come back, an' all I axed 'em was not to hurt 'em if they could help it." Then she broached the point at issue herself.

"I s'pose you've heerd about the fight this mornin'?"

"Yes."

"I reckon you know my boys is hurt—mebbe they're dead in the woods somewhar now." She spoke with little sadness and with no animus whatever. There was no use trying to conceal my purpose

Man-Hunting in the Pound

down there—I saw that at once—and I got up to leave. She would not let me pay for the buttermilk.

"Ef you git hold of 'em—I wish you wouldn't harm 'em," she said, as I climbed on the gray mule, and I promised her that if they were caught unharmed, no further harm should come to them; and I rode away, the group sitting motionless and watching me.

For two hours I ambled along the top of a spur, on a pretty shaded road with precipitous woods on each side, and now and then an occasional cabin, but not a human being was in sight—not for long. Sometimes I would see a figure flitting around a corner of a cabin; sometimes a door would open a few inches and close quickly; and I knew the whole region was terrorized. For two hours I rode on through the sunlight and beauty of those lonely hills, and then I came on a crowd of mountaineers all armed with Winchesters, and just emerging from a cabin by the roadside. It was one division of the searching party, and I joined them. They were much amused when they saw the Christmas toy with which I was armed.

"S'pose one o' the Flemings had stepped out'n the bushes an' axed ye what ye was doin' down hyeh—what would ye 'a' said?"

That might have been embarrassing, and I had to laugh. I really had not thought of that.

One man showed me the Winchester they had captured—Heenan's gun. Tied to the meat-house and leaping against a rope-tether was a dog—which, too, they had captured—Heenan's dog. As we started out the yard " Gooseneck " John Branham, with a look of disgust at my pistol, whipped out one of his own— some two feet long—for me to swing on my other hip. Another fellow critically took in my broad-brim straw hat.

"Hell!" he said. "That won't do. They can see that a mile through the woods. I'll get ye a hat." And he went back into the cabin and brought out a faded slouch-hat.

"That's Heenan's!" he said. That, too, they had captured.

And so I wore Heenan's hat—looking for Heenan.

Half a mile down the road we stepped aside twenty yards into the bushes. There was the cave in which the outlaws had lived. There were in it several blankets, a little bag of meal, and some bits of ham. Right by the side of the road was a huge pile of shavings, where the two outlaws had whittled away many a sunny hour. Half an hour on, down a deep ravine

Man-Hunting in the Pound

and up a long slope, and we were on a woody knoll where the fight had taken place that morning. The little trees looked as though a Gatling gun had been turned loose on them.

The posse had found out where the Flemings were, the night before, by capturing the old Fleming mother while she was carrying them a bag of provisions. As they lay in the brush, she had come along, tossing stones into the bushes to attract the attention of her sons. One of the men had clicked the slide of his Winchester, and the poor old woman, thinking that was the signal from one of her boys, walked toward them, and they caught her and kept her prisoner all night in the woods. Under her apron, they found the little fellow who had lain like a snake in the grass beside me back at the cabin, and, during the night, he had slipped away and escaped and gone back to the county-seat, twenty miles away, on foot, to tell his father, who was a prisoner there, what was taking place at home.

At daybreak, when the posse was closing in on the Flemings, the old woman sprang suddenly to her feet and shouted shrilly: "Run down the holler, boys; run down the holler!"

The ways of rude men, naturally, are not gentle, and the sheriff sprang out and caught the old woman by the throat and choked her cries; and they led her to the rear—weeping and wringing her hands.

A few minutes later, as the men slipped forward through the woods and mist, they came upon the Flemings crouched in the bushes, and each creeping for a tree. "Gooseneck" John Branham—so called because of the length of his neck—Doc Swindall and Ed Hall opened fire. For twenty minutes those two Fleming boys fought twenty-two men fiercely.

"Just looked like one steady flame was a-comin' out o' each man's Winchester all the time," said Branham, pointing to two bullet-pecked trees behind which the outlaws had stood. "I was behind this birch," laying his hand on a tree as big as his thigh, and pointing out where the Flemings had drilled three bullet-holes in it between his neck and his waistband.

"I seed Jim Hale pokin' his gun around this hyeh tree and pumpin' it off inter the ground," said Hall, "an' I couldn't shoot for laughin'."

"Well," said Swindall, "I was tryin' to git in a shot from the oak there, and something struck me and knocked me out in the bushes. I looked around, and damn me if there wasn't seven full-grown men behind my tree."

It had evidently been quite warm for a while, until Branham caught Heenan in the shoulder with a load of buckshot. Heenan's hat went off, his gun dropped to his feet; he cried simply:

"Oh——you!" Then he ran.

Cal Fleming, too, ran then, and the posse fired after them. The dog, curiously enough, lay where he had lain during the fight, at the base of Heenan's tree—and so hat, dog, and gun were captured. I had wondered why the posse had not pursued the Flemings after wounding them, and I began to understand. They were so elated at having been in a fight and come out safe, that they stopped to cook breakfast, gather mementoes, and talk it all over.

Ten minutes later we were at the cabin, where the fugitives had stopped to get some coffee.

"They was pretty badly hurt, I reckon," said the woman who had given them something to eat. "Heenan's shoulder was all shot up, an' I reckon I could git my hand into a hole in Cal's back. Cal was groanin' a good deal, an' had to lay down every ten yards."

We went on hurriedly, and in an hour we struck the main body of the searching party, and as soon as the sheriff saw me, he came running forward. Now, the guard at the Gap had such a reputation that any member of it was supposed to be past-master in the conduct of such matters as were now pending. He immedi-

Blue-grass and Rhododendron

ately called me "Captain," and asked me to take charge of the party. I looked round at them, and I politely veered from the honor. Such a tough-looking gang it has rarely been my good luck to see, and I had little doubt that many of them were worse than the Fleming boys. One tall fellow particularly attracted my attention; he was fully six and one-half feet high; he was very slender, and his legs and arms were the longest I have ever seen swung to a human frame. He had sandy hair, red eyes, high cheek-bones, and on each cheek was a diminutive boil. About his waist was strapped a huge revolver, and to the butt of this pistol was tied a big black bow-ribbon —tied there, no doubt, by his sweetheart, as a badge of death or destruction to his enemies. He looked me over calmly.

"Hev you ever searched for a dead man?" he asked deeply.

It was humiliating to have to confess it in that crowd, but I had not—not then.

"Well, I hev," he said, significantly.

I had little doubt, and for one, perhaps, of his own killing.

In the hollow just below us was the cabin of Parson Swindall—a friend of the Flemings. The parson thought the outlaws dying or dead, and he knew the

"Hev you ever searched for a dead man?"

Man-Hunting in the Pound

cave to which they must have dragged themselves to die. If I got permission from the old Fleming mother, he would guide me, he said, to the spot. I sent back a messenger, promising that the bodies of her sons should not be touched, if they were dead, nor should they be further harmed if they were still alive. The fierce old woman's answer came back in an hour.

"She'd ruther they rotted out in the woods."

Next morning I stretched the men out in a long line, thirty feet apart, and we started on the search. I had taken one man and spent the night in the parson's cabin hoping that, if only wounded, the Flemings might slip in for something to eat; but I had a sleepless, useless night. Indeed, the search had only a mild interest and no excitement. We climbed densely thicketed hills, searched ravines, rocks, caves, swam the river backward and forward, tracking suspicious footsteps in the mud and through the woods. I had often read of pioneer woodcraft, and I learned, during these three days, that the marvellous skill of it still survives in the Southern mountains.

It was dangerous work; dangerous for the man who should run upon the outlaws, since these would be lying still to hear anyone approach them, and would thus "have the drop" from ambush. Once, to be sure, we came near a tragedy. At one parting of two roads several of us stopped to decide which road we should take. At that moment the Fleming boys were lying in the bushes twenty yards away, with their Winchesters cocked and levelled at us over a log, and only waiting for us to turn up that path to open fire. As I was told afterward, Heenan, very naturally, had his Winchester pointed on his hat, which, at that moment, was on my head. By a lucky chance I decided to take the other path. Otherwise, I should hardly be writing these lines to-day.

For three days we searched, only to learn, or rather to be told, which was not the truth, that, in women's dress, the Flemings had escaped over into Kentucky. As a matter of fact, they lay two weeks in a cave, Cal flat on his back and letting the water from the roof of the cave drip, hour by hour, on a frightful wound in his breast.

For several months they went uncaptured, until finally three of the men who were with me, "Gooseneck" John Branham, Ed Hall, and Doc Swindall, located them over the border in West Virginia. Of course a big reward was offered for each, or they were "rewarded," as the mountaineers say. The three men closed in on them in a little store one morning.

Man-Hunting in the Pound

Cal Fleming was reading a letter when the three surged in at the door, and Hall, catching Cal by the lapel of his coat, said quietly:

"You are my prisoner."

Cal sprang back to break the hold, and Hall shot him through the breast, killing him outright. Heenan, who was not thought to be dangerous, sprang at the same instant ten feet away, and his first shot caught Hall in the back of the head, dropping the officer to his knees. Thinking he had done for Hall, Heenan turned on Branham and Swindall, and shot Branham through both lungs and Swindall through the neck—dropping both to the floor. This left the duel between Hall on his knees and Heenan. At last a lucky shot from Hall's pistol struck Heenan's pistol hand, lacerating the fingers and making him drop his weapon. Heenan ran into the back room then, and, finding no egress, reappeared in the doorway, with his bloody hands above his head.

"Well, Ed," he said, simply, "I can't do no more."

Six months later Heenan Fleming was brought back to the county-seat to be tried for his life, and I felt sure that he would meet his end on the scaffold where Talton Hall and Red Fox had suffered death.

As he sat there in the prisoner's box, his face pale

and flecked with powder, I could see a sunken spot in his jaw, through which one of Hall's bullets had gone, and his bright, black eyes gleamed fire. I stepped up to him. I thought there was no chance of his escaping the gallows; but, if he did escape, I wanted to be as friendly with him as possible.

"Heenan," I said, "did you ever get your hat back?"

"No," he said.

"Well, if you come clear, go up to the store and get the best hat in the house, and have it charged to me."

Heenan smiled.

Now, by a curious chance, the woman on whose testimony the Red Fox had been hanged, had died meanwhile. Some people said she had been purposely put out of the way to avoid further testimony. At any rate, through her death, Heenan did come clear, and the last time I saw him, he was riding out of the town on a mule, with his baby in front of him and on his head a brand-new derby hat—mine.

CPSIA information can be obtained
at www.ICGtesting.com
Printed in the USA
LVHW021228160323
741693LV00042B/2159